SKIING
SCHOOL

SKIING
SCHOOL

MARK HELLER

BARRON'S

New York · Toronto

A QUARTO BOOK

First edition for the United States published 1987
by Barron's Educational Series, Inc.

All inquiries should be addressed to:
Barron's Educational Series, Inc.
250 Wireless Boulevard
Hauppauge, New York 11788

International Standard Book No. 0-8120-5836-4

Library of Congress Catalog Card No. 86-32298

Library of Congress Cataloging-in-Publication Data
Heller, Mark F.
  Skiing school.

  Includes index.
  I. Skis and skiing.   I. Title.
GV854.H437 1987   796.93'07   86-32298
ISBN 0.8120-5836-4

This book was designed and produced by
Quarto Publishing plc
The Old Brewery, 6 Blundell Street
London N7 9BH

Senior editor: Stephen Paul
Consultant editor: Doug Godlington, technical advisor
to BASI (British Association of Ski Instructors)
Editor: Donna Dailey

Art editor: Nick Clark
Designers: Julian Dorr, Robin Nicholl, Mick Brennan

Illustrators: Graham Hill, Frazer Numan
Photographer: Clive 'Snaps' Boden

Art director: Pete Laws
Editorial director: Jim Miles

Typeset by Dimension Typesetting, London and
QV Typesetting Ltd, London
Manufactured in Hong Kong by Regent Publishing
Services Limited
Printed by Lee Fung Asco Printers Ltd, Hong Kong

Quarto Publishing would like to thank BASI for their
generous assistance inthe production of this book, and
in particular **Roy Bisset** who demonstrated the
downhill techniques so professionally.
In addition, Quarto Publishing would like to thank
Bladon Lines Travel Limited for providing the
travel and accommodation facilities used for the
location photography in Verbier, Switzerland.

INTRODUCTION

The acquisition of new physical skills in adult life can be difficult and frustrating. When these skills are associated with a hostile environment such as snow, mountains and awkward, cumbersome equipment, the psychological aversion to the activity can negate any constructive attempt to overcome the problems. Skiing is just such a sport, and it is due to the skilled work of the qualified instructors of the skiing countries that the success rate today is more than 80 percent — a figure in excess of that achieved in other sports.

To some beginners the difficulties can appear to be insurmountable: you are asked to slide down an apparent precipice with no visible means of control; instructed to lean away from the safe hillside toward an abyss; required to identify your weight distribution through apparently insensitive and cumbersome boots; and made to bend your body into strange positions. However, once these first critical days are survived, the instructions become reassuringly more comprehensible, performable and satisfying, and those awkward boots begin to display their properties of support and comfort.

But it is not only the beginner who is confronted with this conflict between instinct, skill and technique. The instinctive reactions become modified in the course of practice and experience, but the gap between acquired skill and theoretical technique can become unbridgeable until, as a reasonably proficient moderate skier, the pupil, tired of unremitting instruction defects from ski school to pursue alone or with friends a vain pursuit of excellence while doing nothing more than practice interminably errors and bad habits.

It is a problem which, despite innumerable International Conference decisions to adopt a uniform international teaching standard, is still saddled with an apparent incompatibility between the various national ski schools. A pupil moving from Verbier may well find that what was right there is wrong in La Plagne and laughed at in Mayrhofen, viewed with incredulity by Vail or Killington, and useless on the steep slopes of Taos.

Each national ski school has devised its own progression of instruction, its own vocabulary of shorthand commands and its own distinctive style; and, however apparently different these approaches may seem, it is impossible to identify the schooling history of the accomplished, expert skier. In the end, skill has almost caught up with the techniques which the physical properties of modern skis require for the performance of any given skiing maneuver. At one end of the scale are the numerous paths of entry to the sport skills, and at the other there are the actual performances of the ultimate exponents, the international competitors in downhill, giant slalom and slalom races; the means may differ but the result is indistinguishable.

The past three years have seen a noticeable unification among the once openly hostile, competing schools. France has almost abandoned its *ruade*, though the French ski instructor is still inclined to start a run with *'alors, tout gentiment, Hop, Hop'* and then to disappear round a corner, ski tails high in the air.

Austria has reluctantly attempted to abandon its hallmark "comma" position by disguising it with leg angulation but its instructors have never lived down Professor Kruckenhauser's graphic counter-rotation movements, as illustrated by his sequence pictures of children.

North America faces an entirely different problem. Every single resort is a complex of two or more financial and commercial interests, and thus pressure is brought to bear on the ski schools to get their customers onto the lifts fast. In achieving this they have abandoned old tenets and possibly too fervently embraced the psychological by-ways of instruction theory. On the plus side, however, is the abundance of multi-level trails which provide good skiing for skiers of varying abilities and allow beginners immediate safe running away from the confines of the beginners' slopes.

When work on this book was started it was expected that a forest of contradictions and a welter of idiosyncracies would be encountered. What in fact was discovered was a semantic jungle and an inevitable attempt to analyze in a series of verbal high-speed freeze frames a flowing, interdependent, complex of visible and invisible actions that defy a meaningful description.

One day, soon, an enterprising authority is going to produce the ultimate video instruction series; using every electronic trick and device, we will be able to see foot pressures in located Technicolor, body flexes with superimposed force diagrams and, possibly, psychological stress patterns. It will be so complete and so perplexing that it will discourage the beginner for life.

This book is intended to serve as a guide through this confusing progression. It is not a teach-yourself manual — you cannot learn to ski through a book. But you can learn to understand what is being taught, why it is being taught and how you can more easily apply the demonstrated techniques, body positions and weight commands to your individual requirements.

CONTENTS

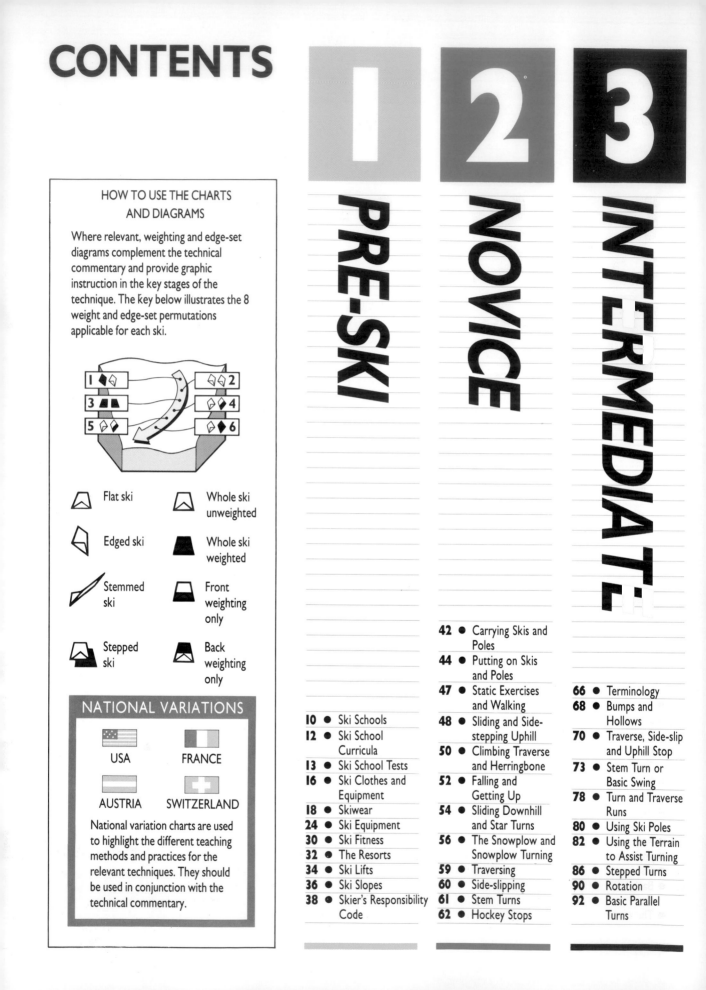

1 PRE-SKI

2 NOVICE

3 INTERMEDIATE

HOW TO USE THE CHARTS AND DIAGRAMS

Where relevant, weighting and edge-set diagrams complement the technical commentary and provide graphic instruction in the key stages of the technique. The key below illustrates the 8 weight and edge-set permutations applicable for each ski.

1
3
5

2
4
6

Flat ski	Whole ski unweighted
Edged ski	Whole ski weighted
Stemmed ski	Front weighting only
Stepped ski	Back weighting only

NATIONAL VARIATIONS

USA   FRANCE

AUSTRIA   SWITZERLAND

National variation charts are used to highlight the different teaching methods and practices for the relevant techniques. They should be used in conjunction with the technical commentary.

PRE-SKI

Skiing is a free-ranging equipment-dependent sport comparable in many ways to sailing, with as many sub-disciplines — recreational, competitive, amateur, professional, resort skiing or ski touring and mountaineering. But unlike sailing, ski equipment is foreign to most people, the clothing is highly specialized and the mountain slopes and even glaciers, based on adapted or specially constructed villages, are for the novice skier a rather alienating environment.

The sophistication that the skiing world has adopted can be so overwhelming that the novice is often at a complete loss, confused by the well meant suggestions of self-proclaimed experts, embarrassed by the offers of second-hand and out-of-date clothes and equipment, and incapacitated by attempting to decide between the enormous range of resorts and services. That such problems exist is not altogether a bad thing since they help to underline the seriousness of the sport and emphasize the need to be well prepared. Mountain winters place a severe strain on even highly specialized clothing, and modern skiing techniques demand the highest level of sophistication from boots, bindings and skis — in short, the sport depends, in its present state of development, on the fullest use of high technology. Skis are not just planks of wood but engineered products with which skiing is made acceptably easy for the casual recreational skier, and today's designs have reduced the average learning time from years to weeks. The villages, whether old conventional mountain communities or modern purpose-built ski centers, must be well organized if the expense of living there is to be repaid by efficient and convenient skiing amenities.

Every sport likes to think of itself as special, imbued with its own mystique and resentful of ill-informed, outside intrusion. No one is more vocal and aggressive than the newly infected skier who has discovered an entirely new world. Skiing is no longer a class-conscious, exclusive pastime but is instantly available from the plethora of skiing tour operators — but with a proviso! Because it is a true sport, even if not athletically exclusive, much disillusion can be prevented if the approach is a little more informed and the actual first slide on snow not quite such a physical and psychological shock. The better prepared you are the more you will enjoy your skiing and the more technically proficient you will become.

SKI SCHOOLS

Every sport has its teaching, training and pedagogic hierarchy, but there is none that is so structured, conservative, restrictive and numerous as the sport of skiing. If you accept that every ski resort has a ski school of some size or other and that there are about 3,000 such ski resorts world-wide, and that they employ 10 qualified instructors, you have a small army of at least 30,000 salaried, winter-months-employed persons engaged in the teaching of skiing. Since there are known to be about 10 times the number of such qualified instructors who do not work full-time, the total number of people theoretically entitled to take you onto the snow and attempt to teach you how to ski must be close to half a million.

Furthermore, it takes about three years to qualify as a ski instructor, of which at least two are spent as apprentice teachers. To complete such a course, which includes probably a lengthy period under academic instruction, costs about $10,000 in terms of fees, accommodation and equipment, not all of which is subsidized, and the chances of earning that much in a single season are slim.

THE BEGINNINGS Strangely, perhaps, the teaching of skiing has always attracted some quite outstanding personalities. The first recorded was a Norwegian regular army captain, Jens Emahusen of Trondheim, who also wrote a booklet for his troops summarizing his very simple skiing precepts in 1733 — Norwegian troops had first been organized into ski units in 1716. It was not until Sondre Norheim demonstrated his revolutionary style in 1868 in Christiania (Oslo) that there is any further record of an organized ski school. Norheim and his companions from Morgedal, the brothers Hemmestveit, started a school in Morgedal but it appears to have lasted only one winter.

Mathias Zdarsky is probably the true founder of the ski school, much as we now know it. He set up a military-style school in Lilienfeld near Vienna in 1896 where he drilled his pupils, both civilian and military, with Prussian-like discipline. It was from this line of pupils that the really constructive teaching of skiing developed. Here pioneers like Sohm, Bilgeri and Rickmers learned their craft and, in their turn, gave rise to new and adventurous generations of ski innovators, most notably Hannes Schneider from the Arlberg (Austria) and Vivian Caulfield, a British engineer by training, who wrote a revolutionary ski instruction manual in 1911 called *How to Ski and Not to Ski*.

HANNES SCHNEIDER It was, however, Hannes Schneider who conceived the basis for what we now know as "the ski school" for recreational skiers. He laid down the teaching precepts, the organization of classes, supervision of instructors and standardization of methods of instruction. This was during the years 1907-18. In 1920 he collaborated with Dr. Fanck in the making of a most historic ski film *Das Wunder des Schneeschuhs* (The Marvel of Skis). It had a dramatic effect in Germany, Austria and Switzerland but was completely ignored by the wider skiing public.

During the 1920s, in resorts where there were a number of British skiers, the Ski Club of Great Britain, with the occasional help of local skiers, undertook the teaching of basic skiing on an entirely voluntary, amateur basis. In certain resorts, one or more large hotels employed amateurs to teach their guests skiing and to organize ski expeditions. It was a haphazard kind of organization which led, inevitably, to the creation of commercial "schools" in certain villages.

It is impossible to fix a date to the creation of controlled, licensed ski schools in the Alps. There is little doubt that the origins lay with the Austrian villages, based on the "Arlberg School," and in Switzerland with the creation first of the village authorities, then cantonal organizations and finally federal control by a statutory federal organization.

Unlike other countries at that time, that is to say the 1930s and late 1940s, Switzerland tended to develop two or more competing schools in the same village — a pattern that was to remain in St Moritz and Zermatt until late in the 1970s.

THE MODERN SKI SCHOOL Today all countries' ski schools are based on a single National Ski School Federation which in turn subscribes to an international body, the International Ski Instructors Association (ISIA), founded in 1951 in Zurs, Austria. The ISIA holds regular "Interski" conferences whose aim is to promote uniformity, a task now well on its complicated and strife-torn path to success.

It must, however, always suffer from the fact that the teaching of skiing and the running of schools is a commercial undertaking, a fact which all too often is forgotten by those who administer organizations. Inevitably a degree of nationalism creeps into the teaching, especially when one particular nationality has been successful in international ski championships. Thus in the early 1950s, Sailer, Austria, supplanted the French dominance of Allais and Vuarnet and the Austrian schools produced a sanitized version of the Sailer style while the French continued to preach their *ruade* initiation of parallels which, for the pupil, was in complete contradiction to the smooth, shoulder-rotation style. At times this nationalism reached bizarre levels, notably during the Austrian "comma" position for traverse running which was an attempt to ease the problems of learning to traverse on the equipment of the time, and which hallmarked any Austrian-taught skier.

Today, things are much simpler. The differences are either specific and positive or they are merely a case of emphasis, caused largely by the development in equipment from the soft boots and stiff skis of the 1950s to the stiff boots and soft skis of the 1980s. In any event, the end product is barely distinguishable. The differences lie more in organization and character. Thus the French still tend to concentrate more on private tuition, leaving group teaching to the beginner classes and to the infant groups. They are also much more concerned with performance skiing rather than recreational cruising. The Austrians, recently, have been concentrating on smoothness and roundness in their turns, aiming principally to teach style at a relatively early stage. The Swiss under the creative pressure of their technical director, Karl Gamma, are concerned with teaching their visitors to enjoy their skiing as early in their pupilage as possible. The American approach is influenced by the pressure of commercialism; it is imperative that they get their pupils lift-skiable as soon as possible, as in lift ticket sales lies the road to profitability. But they are also eager learners and are concerned with skiing correctly while being aware of their public's demand for instant success and instant skill.

GLM The nature of the profession encourages a degree of conservatism and a reluctance to abandon time-honored procedures. Thus it was the ski teaching profession which fought a useless rearguard action against short skis, arguing that it would never teach people to ski "real skis." Innovation in the form of the GLM system proved them to be wrong, even though the GLM method in its original form died through commercial pressure from the ski equipment retailers (the complications of holding stocks of different ski lengths so that pupils could change as they progressed proved to be too costly). But it left behind the convincing proof that to ski well it was not necessary to use skis 2.4m (7ft 10in) long. Similarly, ski teachers world-wide found that the old custom of making the school class a strong social unit for the duration of the ski holiday was an unbearable invasion of their free time and a positive disruption of their family life. It gradually died out but today, faced with a declining number of pupils in the higher classes, both Austria and Switzerland are actively studying ways of re-introducing that most admirable social unit — the ski school class.

There may be many things wrong with today's ski schools but it must be admitted that they are carrying out the role the skiing public have assigned them. Ski schools exist to teach people to ski as quickly as possible and it is a great mark in their favor that over 80 percent of their pupils are satisfied.

*Games and competitions are an important part of children's ski school classes **above**, not least because they help relieve the boredom of some of the more routine exercises.*

SKI SCHOOL CURRICULA

All ski schools organize their classes in accordance with the skill levels of their pupils and a generalized outline of the intended curriculum. Since, theoretically at least, a class should not be larger than 12 pupils and ideally not more than eight and, wherever possible, instruction should be given in the native language of the pupils, it follows that individual class levels will often be duplicated. Within such duplication there will also be an often well-defined difference in skill and enthusiasm. So it is not at all uncommon to find that a given class level will subdivide into "good" or "fast" classes and "low" classes.

As an indication of the skills theoretically taught in given classes as well as some help to pupils in making a self-assessment, the following tables, taken from the official ski instructors' handbooks, may help.

THE AMERICAN METHOD

Class A
Moving on the level
Sliding on a grade

Class B
Direction changes

Class C
Skidded turns

Class D
Widetrack turning

Class E
Carved turning
Rebound turning

Class F
All snow — All terrain

THE FEDERAL AUSTRIAN SKI SCHOOL

Class 6
Familiarization with equipment
Static exercises
Sliding straight (*Schuss*)
Traversing
Herringbone and side-step climbing

Class 5
Simple ski lift use
Snowplow
Snowplow turning

Class 4
Up-ski stem turns
Down-ski stem turns
Uphill turns
Side-slipping

Class 3
Linked turns
Basic parallels

Class 2
Advanced parallels
Basic stepped parallels

Class 1
Racing turns
Powder snow
Short swings
Slalom practice

FRENCH NATIONAL SKI SCHOOL

Class Debutants (Beginners)
Familiarization
Walking and balance on the flat
Initiation into ski lift use
First downhill sliding on shortish skis
Children: Gliding snowplow
Basic snowplow turn

Class 1
Basic snowplow turn
Side slipping
Introduction to stem turns
Children: Traverse
Basic stem turning
Side-slipping

Class 2
Basic parallel turn
Basic short swing
Children: Parallels
Fast straight running

Class 3
Fast skiing on all kinds of slopes
Moguls
Initiation to slalom skiing
Children: Slalom
Short swings

Competition
Slalom and Giant Slalom

SWISS SKI SCHOOL

Class 1
Familiarization
Falling and standing up
Walking
Climbing — side-stepping and traverse
Climbing
Straight sliding
Snowplow gliding
Stepping around

Class 2
Snowplow turns
Ski lift and chair-lift basics
Traversing
Side-slipping and uphill turns
Linked snowplow turns
Basic introduction to step turns

Class 3
Kick turns
Skating steps
Bumps and hollows
Basic stem turns
Uphill turns

Class 4
Basic parallels with up-unweighting
Basic parallels with down-unweighting
Basic parallels with bump assistance

Class 5
Basic short swings
Stepped parallels
High speed bumps and hollows and jumps

Class 6
Advanced short swings
Racing turns
Powder snow skiing
Difficult, off-slope skiing

SKI SCHOOL TESTS

There cannot be a skier who has not, at one time or another, had to subject himself or herself to the pleasure, excitement, horror, fear or just plain boredom of the weekly ski school tests. And, in due course, those who have submitted (and paid) for their tests get a badge, a certificate and a round of applause.

THE HISTORY OF TESTS Ski school tests were originally devised by the Ski Club of Great Britain in 1920 to provide a means of obtaining a more or less objective standard of ski performance, on the basis of which it would be possible to determine who was and who was not fit to take on a ski trip without causing any personal offense. As a fall-out from this categorization, the tests would also assist in recruiting membership among the increasing number of individual skiers who, as yet, owed no allegiance to any ski organization.

The concept of the three categories of skiers — the novice, third class, bronze badge; the intermediate, second class, silver badge; and finally the expert, first class, gold badge — has stayed with us ever since and even though the requirements are now vastly different from what they were originally, they are still a valid basis for ski performance judgment.

TEST REQUIREMENTS The ski skill requirements have also not varied greatly in principle. The lowest category, bronze, examined the skier's capability of what is today called the "turn-and-traverse" technique using basic snowplow and/or stem turns. Falls were discouraged and led to disqualification as did excessively slow skiing. The silver qualification examined the degree of fluency (and to this end required the skiing of a standard course within a given time), the performance of more advanced turns (in those days "Telemarks") and the ability to perform with some degree of fluency on varied or difficult snow — a fairly obvious requirement in the days before prepared slopes. The gold requirements were very much higher, requiring both speed and fluency in every kind of snow and a degree of downhill racing ability. What this all amounted to was the knowledge that you could take a silver badge skier off on a day's ski trip with no qualms as to his or her performance while the gold skier could bask in a publicly acknowledged expertise. The performance levels were, perforce, subjective and were assessed by two or even three independent and qualified judges. The service was free to all members as it still is today, although now there is greater emphasis on time qualification

Ski school tests **right** *are an integral part of the modern teaching progression. The bronze, silver and gold badges are a great incentive and are proudly worn as proof of technical expertise.*

through a standard slalom or giant slalom course. (However, there remains, unique to the British tests, the subjective assessment of the silver and gold candidates in terms of fluency and steadiness in all forms of snow, while in the Rockies potential helicopter skiers are given a powder snow test before being allowed to make the trip.)

Serious reference to these SCGB ski tests is justified, for they have formed, world-wide, the basis for the many varieties of ski school tests which are carried out today by every ski school in the world. Which school was the first to adapt these British tests it is difficult, if not impossible, to determine but it seems likely that the Arlberg first introduced them as part of their normal school class social habit. Here, again divided into the three classical grades, the class instructor awarded the badges on the basis of personal, subjective assessment. It was the Swiss ski schools who were probably the first to devise a more objective form of assessment by means of semi-competitive slalom tests and to levy a payment for the tests which required both time and money to organize. The French schools were the first to devise two parallel sets of tests — one a conforming, more or less standard performance test and another which was openly competitive. It was left to North America to refine the whole confusion of disparate qualifications into one single, commercially sponsored, performance test, the NASTAR. This has since been copied recently in Austria and a similar kind of nation-wide test, applicable particularly to artificial slopes and the teaching of children, has been available in Britain for several years.

Today's performance tests, with the exception of the infant grades, are all based on what could be termed a standard slalom which has a standard time set by an instructor. Candidates are required to ski the slalom, unseen, within a given percentage time of the "standard." Allowance is made for age and experience. For the more advanced tests, a standard giant slalom type of course is used. An outright downhill is neither feasible nor practical and ski schools have enough trouble finding a free slope for the existing types of test courses. Many resorts are now building and preparing special, fenced courses for just this purpose.

TEST ORGANIZATION In Switzerland and Austria the organization of school tests is a matter concerning only the local ski school director; there is no central administration though in Switzerland the Association of Swiss Ski Schools and the Swiss Ski Federation have agreed on a form of standardization and a common test badge. Austria, within each provincial ski organization (ie. Tirol, Vorarlberg, Salzburg etc) maintains a similar general advisory role. In France, the Ecole de Ski France (ESF) controls the standards and classifications. In North America, apart from the NASTAR races, it is up to each individual ski school to introduce standards; in practice few have done so, though the Professional Ski

Instructors of America have recently introduced a "Standard Rating" (STAR) test with bronze, silver and gold categories. These are subjective tests based on skill and fluency in novice, intermediate and expert slope skiing, including powder snow in the expert category.

The WISBI races (Austria) This is an acronym for *"Wie Schnell Bin Ich?"* ("How fast am I?"). The organization, nationally based, is similar to all slalom-type tests, where a standard course is skied against a standard time. The test is a direct descendant of the NASTAR races.

The NASTAR (North America) First introduced in North America in the winter of 1968-69, this very popular National Standard Race was thought up by the American *Ski Magazine* to enable amateurs to assess their ability and skill progress nationwide. The compe-

The excitement of children's races **left** is really infectious. Even the tiniest of entrants behaves with all the style of a fully-fledged international racer and they can hardly wait to hurl themselves through the starting gate.

titor's time is registered as a percentage of the "official" time for the course and this is standardized by age and sex. There are, as customary, three grades — bronze, silver and gold. To make certain that conditions are standardized, there is an annual pace-setters meeting where each designated pace-setter skis the same course 10 times. The pacesetter is then handicapped against the average of his times and those of the other pace-setters. On returning to his resort, this pace time is then amended by the amount of the handicap. The test is sponsored annually by a major commercial interest and the number of resorts that are authorized to run NASTAR races is limited.

The French tests The Ecole de Ski France runs three sets of tests. The *Etoile* (snowflake) star has four categories — infant, first, second and third star. These are standard ski school class awards up to about interme-

diate standard. Rather more prestigious is the *Chamois* series — bronze, silver, scarlet and gold. These are combined performance tests which include a timed slalom but also demand a high standard of on-and-off-slope skiing. The award of the gold *Chamois* is something of an honor and relatively rare. A purely racing award is the *Flèche* (Arrow), also in four categories, and based on pure slalom and/or giant slalom racing performance. Both the *Flèche* and the *Chamois* are taken extremely seriously by French skiers who will undertake many hours of private instruction in order to reach the very high standard required. Of all the commercialized skiing awards, it would seem at the moment that only the *Chamois* deserve direct comparison with the kind of standard set in the Ski Club of Great Britain tests, and a gold *Chamois* holder is probably slightly superior in performance to a British gold test.

SKI CLOTHES AND EQUIPMENT

You can play golf in virtually any outfit you choose. You can play tennis or football or go fishing dressed as you please, provided that you are comfortable, cool or warm and your feet are adequately protected and suitable for your pursuit. Once upon a time much the same applied to skiing — within limits. In the 1920s it was most unconventional not to wear a tie with your flannel shirt under your tweed jacket.

However, as the sport grew in popularity it soon became apparent that rather more attention was required as to the kind of clothes you wore and the kind of boots you clamped into your unyielding bear-trap bindings. As skiers ventured higher and farther into the mountains, specialized wind- and snow-proof clothes, boots with special heels and squared-off toes and gloves that kept you both warm and dry and let you hold your ski poles with some degree of conviction had to be designed, invented, marketed and finally sold to the novice skier. These demands soon gave birth to a quite recognizable fashion and, reading the advertisements of those years, it is obvious that the first ski equipment and clothing manufacturers had taken the trouble to inquire into the requirements of these new customers. The garments may well look strange and impractical to us now, but for their day they were well made, serviceable and fashionable.

It was not until the 1950s that any real attempt was made to create genuine ski fashions. The beginnings were simple — tight, semi-elasticized trousers, the famous "Vorlage" Helanca stretch pants which were to become everyday wear; the wind- and waterproof jacket that soon acquired the Eskimo name "Anorak," a virtually world-wide uniform of daily wear; and the hard, specialized boots with steel-strengthened soles that could withstand the compression pressures of the newly invented safety bindings. These were enough to set the skier apart from most other sportsmen, if only by reason of the cost of the specially made items of equipment.

The advent of what could be called "high technology" (for that apparently distant age) brought a completely new aspect to the problem of equipping yourself adequately for the slopes. The first really big innovation was the invention, by Henke of Switzerland, of the clip boot which put an end to blistered and cracked fingers and the interminable struggle to lace up boots. The reasons were really twofold: to make suitable ski boots out of leather was becoming impossible on a production-line basis; and to make a plastic-shelled boot which could be laced was an engineering disaster.

The development of ski clothing was, however, more successful. Artificial fibers and the growing importance of the market attracted top French designers; bright and cheerful colors finally banished the drab blues and blacks; and new shapes, cuts and ideas gradually supplanted the accustomed jacket and pants combination. Boot makers finally realized that human beings had to wear their contraptions for long hours every day — and even more important, that the human foot is capable of more variations than the standard size tabulations allowed for.

What the future holds for ski clothing is open to speculation but one thing is certain; there can be no other sport that has had so large an influence on everyday leisure wear. Generally speaking, you would not go shopping in an Ellesse tennis outfit or go for a country walk dressed by Spalding for golf. However, go shopping on a winter's day wearing your latest investment in ski jackets, shod in moonboots and with your hands warmed by the reflected glow of a pair of Thinsulate ski mitts and you will be regarded as well dressed. The only objection to this happy state of affairs is the possibly immoderate costs of such high-fashion garments. This objection is at least partially offset, however, by the fact that you can now comprehensively equip yourself for skiing in your nearest sports clothing store and rest assured in the knowledge that whatever you buy has been the result of years of research and development.

*The ski racer's clothes **left** are designed primarily for speed. Tight-fitting and visually dynamic, they are subject to the same degree of research and development that is lavished on boots and skis. Recreational skiwear **above** has also benefited from this attention, and modern outfits combine the best elements of practicality and style.*

Skiing is today a high-technology sport, and what you wear to practice it must, if you are to be warm, comfortable and socially acceptable, be technically correct. As a skier you will be exposed to a variety of inhospitable circumstances such as great temperature fluctuations, ferocious winds and driving snow and you will often be required to endure a long, cold ride on a wet chair-lift seat. Your boots will have to bear severe tension and compression forces, and still be comfortable to wear for long, hard-working hours. Your skis will not only have to withstand your skiing antics but they must also actively assist you in performing maneuvers. Your bindings will have to cope with seemingly contradictory requirements — to hold your boots on the skis against immense force and yet release you unharmed from a sudden jerk of only minimal force. All this has today been achieved and, what is more, achieved with elegance and, in most cases, within an acceptable budget.

SKIWEAR

*The one-piece racing suit **above** is a figure-hugging outfit designed to reduce wind-resistance without restricting movement.*

The outer layer is the most important — it must be weather-proof and wind-proof, and it must provide warmth without excessive bulk or restriction of movement. Modern skiwear can and for the most part does live up to these governing factors. For years, designers have worked with skiers to create the most practical and acceptable designs. They have influenced fabric manufacturers and inspired the creation of increasingly efficient thermal fills.

Good quality skiwear is highly technical and it can usefully be divided into two categories — high performance and fashion. High performance skiwear is designed for aggressive and demanding skiers who ask a lot from their equipment and who expect it to withstand the severest conditions. Fashion skiwear is geared more towards recreational skiers and spans everything from very expensive, designer creations to the more practical, affordable ranges. With the abundance of versatile modern fabrics, fills and dyes, designers have been able to create an entire fashion scene around ski clothing while sacrificing none of the necessary functional properties.

The most important requirement of all skiwear is that it provides a completely weather-proof exterior on the mountain. It must leave you prepared and protected against any sudden change in the weather (which is, unfortunately, a regular occurrence). With this in mind, choose a garment with an integral hood (which is usually hidden) and a collar which fits snugly around your neck and is high enough to keep out biting winds and snow. All closures should be covered by a fly or over-flap, as snow will quickly penetrate any exposed or unprotected area. In addition, any point where snow can enter such as pockets, wrists and ankles should have an inner cuff which should close tightly by means of snaps, elastic or Velcro.

HOW TO CHOOSE A wise and considered choice of skiwear can make all the difference to your skiing trip. Knowing what to choose from the seemingly endless ranges and combinations currently available can be a daunting task, but there can be no doubt that time spent preparing yourself for skiing will make the actual skiing all the more enjoyable.

The thermal-filled, two-piece suit consisting of a jacket and matching overpants is a popular and practical choice overcoming, as it does, the common problem of snow penetrating at the waistband. A variation on this is the separate jacket combined with contrasting fabric racing-style pants or stretch corduroys. Alternatively, there is the one-piece suit, either in a classic tailored style or designed like a flying suit, the latter being more

generously cut and very comfortable to wear. Whichever you choose, these can be worn with a matching or contrasting vest, adding a second dimension to your basic look as well as extra warmth.

However, it is very important to remember that no matter how attractive you find a particular garment or combination of garments, your primary consideration when choosing *must* be the suitability of the clothing to the severe test that mountain conditions impose. You may wish to be the most stylish skier on the slope, but this will in no way add to your enjoyment of skiing if you are freezing cold and perpetually extracting snow that has penetrated your clothing.

POINTS TO WATCH FOR Always make a point of trying *all* clothing for a good fit in the shop before making your purchase. Bend down to touch your toes to see if there is any tightness across the seat or at the crotch. Then bend at the knees and look out for similar areas of tightness or restricted movement. Likewise, raise your arms above your head and (especially if you are trying a combination suit) check that your waist is not exposed. If you are trying on a one-piece suit, there should be no significant movement between the top and bottom sections. Stretch your arms out in front of you and make sure that the sleeves have not moved so far up your wrists that they are uncomfortable. And lastly put your hands on your hips, pull your elbows forward and then turn your back to the mirror and watch for any stress

Close-fitting cuffs

Snug collar

Integral gaiters

Integral hood

Knee padding

Elasticized waistband

The one-piece suit **top** is an increasingly popular recreational outfit, both comfortable and stylish. A common variation is the separate jacket combined with racing-style pants **above**. Whatever outfit you choose, make sure that it is both weather-proof and wind-proof.

marks at the armhole seams or tightness across the back panel. As a final check, inspect all linings, seams and closures to make sure that there are no obvious defects, and operate any zippers (which should not be so hard to handle that they are impossible to work with cold fingers).

ACCESSORIES Accessories are all those extra items that are both functional and fashionable. However, before buying anything you must be satisfied that it is above all functional.

A woolen sweater is a necessity. Most skiwear designers now produce woolens to team or contrast with their ranges. Modern skiwear works on the principle of built-in warmth, so you do not need a thick and bulky sweater. Different people generate different levels of body heat; those who generate a lot of body heat need fewer layers, while those who tend to feel the cold more should simply add layers until they create the right balance for their particular needs.

Turtleneck sweaters are strongly advised since they not only help in the build up of warmth but also serve to absorb perspiration. The snug fit around the neck helps to trap the warm air that circulates around the body while the material absorbs any moisture and allows it to escape through evaporation, thus permitting the body to breathe. This is a very important function since chilling quickly sets in when the body is damp.

Beneath this layer you can add your personal choice of undergarments, usually an undershirt and/or long johns. Remember, however, that such undergarments should not be too tight; each layer should act as a cell of warm air, and this must be allowed to circulate to keep your skin dry and your body temperature controlled. Overheating during strenuous exertion is just as harmful as chilling.

HEAD AND FACE Scientific investigations show that a high proportion of body heat is lost through the extremities, and in particular the head. You should never go skiing without a hat and gloves, and in extreme cold you should always protect your face, ears and neck. There are sensitive glands around the neck area which will become swollen, stiff and very painful when exposed to the cold. A ski mask is ideal, since it creates a wind-proof seal around the neck and head and also protects most of your face.

FEET The design of modern ski boots is such that thick and bulky socks are not necessary, and in fact the warmth/function/comfort properties that designers have striven to achieve are defeated if the foot is encased in bulk.

There are basically two types of specialist ski socks, either contoured like regular socks or the "ski tube" variety which, as the name suggests, is a shapeless sock that takes on the form of the foot when worn. The latter are definitely preferable since the design ensures that there is no wrinkling or bunching. Whichever you

Regular socks 1, woolen sweater 2, "ski tube" socks 3, turtleneck T-shirt 4, long johns 5, and gaiters 6, are just some of the many accessories you will need.

choose, make sure that you take several pairs with you when you go skiing. Feet become very uncomfortable when imprisoned in worn and tired socks, not least because a dirty sock prevents the foot from breathing. As with the rest of your ski outfit, make sure that your socks are not too tight and that they have not shrunk in the wash and become matted. Any of these factors will hamper proper circulation and will accentuate the problem of cold feet.

At the end of every day's skiing you should wash your feet thoroughly, giving them rather more care and attention than you would normally do. Try and keep your toenails short; they will become very painful and even permanently damaged if you do not.

It cannot be stressed too strongly that it is essential (in terms of safety *and* comfort) that your ski boots fit well. However, if you are unfortunate enough to get painful pressure points on bones or to the skin, do not think you can reduce the problem by wearing extra socks — this will only make it worse. If you cannot change your boots for another pair, then you should relieve the problem by using some surgical padding. Cut away an area a fraction larger in diameter than the affected zone and apply the padding around the sore spot, keeping it in position with your sock.

*Overpants **below** are warm and comfortable, and are a very popular choice.*

*The lined vest **above** is ideal for spring skiing.*

*Bobble hat **1**, leather gloves **2**, thermal liners **3**, and thermal ski mask **4**, all help to reduce heatloss from vulnerable extremities.*

HANDS Always wear gloves or mittens. No matter how sunny and warm the weather looks from the comfort of the resort center, the temperature rapidly drops the higher you get and unprotected hands will very quickly get cold.

When choosing gloves or mittens you should always buy the best you can afford; cheap gloves are a false economy since they offer little protection against the cold and soon wear out. It is always worth taking two pairs of gloves or mittens with you in case one pair gets wet. Good quality leather gloves should be allowed to dry slowly and should never be placed over any form of direct heat. If you do not observe these guidelines the leather will harden and crack and the gloves will lose their waterproof qualities. It is a good idea to treat them regularly with a weather-proofing spray.

On very cold days silk, cotton or thermal liners can be worn. As a matter of routine, you should always carry a pair of liner gloves with you so that if you are unfortunate enough to lose a glove while out on the slope (which can easily happen) you will at least have some means of protecting your exposed hand.

Protection against the cold is not the only reason for wearing gloves or mittens. Snow, as soft and fluffy as it may look, has an abrasive quality, and if you fall with your hands uncovered you will receive a graze similar to that caused by gravel.

EYES AND SKIN Protecting yourself against the mountain elements does not end with clothing. Common sense will help you to keep warm but there are two areas of potential harm which you may not be so readily aware of.

Eyes You must never venture out onto the snow without some form of eye protection, and this means something more than ordinary sunglasses. If you are unsure, go to a specialist ski shop where you will find styles in all shapes and sizes. Remember that light rays will penetrate from the sides, so choose a style that will prevent this.

In bad weather you will need goggles — it is virtually impossible to ski in a blizzard or "white-out" without them, For a white-out you need a special lens color, amber or yellow, to give definition. Some makes have

Goggles and glasses Goggles are absolutely essential for bad weather. Amber or yellow lenses *1* give added definition in a white-out, while pink lenses *2* are suitable for all qualities of light. Skiing sun- glasses should have side-pieces *3* to stop light penetrating from the side. Folding sunglasses *4* are a stylish and space-saving innovation.

detachable lenses to allow for all conditions; others rely on one special lens color, either grey or pink, to compensate for all qualities of light.

In a blizzard, goggles are absolutely vital. Eyes are easily bruised and scratched by driving snow; add to this the speed with which you are moving down the slope and each snowflake becomes a potential missile. To try to combat the bombardment, your eyes will water profusely as nature attempts to clear the foreign objects from them; they will sting and burn and you will be temporarily blinded.

Even when the sun is not shining lasting damage can be done to your eyes by exposure to the high ultraviolet factor found at altitude. The damage is done quickly and silently and it is not until some time later that you become aware of the harm. At the least you will suffer conjunctivitis, at the worst you will suffer snow blindness; both are painful and the latter is usually permanent, affecting the light tolerance of your eyes for the rest of your life.

Skin Your skin also needs its share of care and protection. Sun, snow and breathtakingly fresh air, while being the essential ingredients of any successful skiing trip, are powerful agents that your skin must be prepared for. Sun-and-snow cream is therefore a must, not only to protect your skin but also to replace the natural oils as they are dried out. You should give your skin extra nourishment before, during and after your skiing trip, and you should ensure that it has adequate protection throughout your time on the slope. Apart from any protective considerations this will ensure that your tan lasts longer and your skin glows with health. (You should avoid all alcohol-based facial compounds where possible.)

Sun-and-snow cream comes in several levels of protection — those with extra sensitive skin should use a high protection-factor preparation. Pay special attention to the soft area around the eyes, high spots such as the forehead, nose and cheekbones, then coat the tips and lobes of the ears, under the chin and jaw area, not forgetting your neck. Re-apply before going onto the slopes and top up regularly throughout the day. Use a good lip salve, and renew it constantly to prevent painful and unsightly chapping.

Boot bag and ski bag The safest way of carrying boots, skis and poles when traveling.

Fanny pack Handy for carrying small bits and pieces.

Backpack A convenient way of carrying extra clothing for a day's skiing.

23

SKI EQUIPMENT

Ski equipment is, as mentioned before, generally quite expensive. For this reason many people who are new to the sport prefer to rent the necessary equipment for the first year or two and then, perhaps, buy themselves a pair of boots. However, renting equipment is not necessarily as cheap as you may imagine, and at some point it is well worth calculating the cost of rental over several skiing trips and comparing this against the purchase of a set of equipment. In some French and Swiss resorts a two-week rental can represent as much as 25 percent of the purchase price for the same equipment. If this is where you intend to do most of your skiing, it is worth bearing in mind that a good set of skis, boots and poles will last for many more than eight weeks and will still retain a healthy second-hand value after this. In other countries renting equipment is much cheaper and is, therefore, a more attractive option provided that it is well maintained.

If, after taking these factors into account, you decide to strike a balance between the two options, consider buying second-hand or ex-rental equipment. At the end of each winter season most ski shops have an excellent range of bargains available.

SKI BOOTS The plastic-shelled boot, first introduced in the early 1970s, now monopolizes the market and has enabled recreational skiers worldwide to make very rapid technical progress.

Rigid and supportive, the plastic-shelled boot keeps your feet dry and well insulated from the cold. Unlike an ordinary shoe, it will not soften or stretch in use and only has a lining of foam padding to absorb slight variations in foot shape. For this reason some skiers, whose feet do not conform to the manufacturer's standard tabulations, suffer from pressure points or cramps in their boots. Fortunately such discomforts (which can ruin a skiing trip) can be largely overcome thanks to the ever-growing improvement in fitting techniques. Whether buying or renting boots, you should always take the trouble to shop around, and it is most unlikely that you will not be able to find a comfortable pair somewhere or a shop that will modify a pair to fit.

How they work Ski boots comprise a rigid, plastic outer shell and an inner padded boot. The shell has two functions in helping you to ski. The first is to stiffen the ankle and restrict its lateral "play." In this way your leg movements, forward and sideways, are translated into pressure along the ski's base and edges to produce the steering effect. The second is to point the lower leg forward at an angle of about 15 to 20 degrees from the vertical. This helps you to adopt the correct stance.

The shell is ideally made in three or more parts and is hinged near the ankle joint. The boot is opened either at the back (rear-entry) or by pulling out a tongue (front-entry). The tightness or fit is governed by the quality and quantity of controls or buckles around the shell. These either reduce the volume of the shell or

Boot shell 1, padded inner boot 2, custom-molded insole 3, front-entry racing boot 4, and rear-entry recreational boot 5.

reduce the volume of the inner boot internally through the use of cables, plates or inflatable air bladders.

Various other controls can also help in "tuning" the fit or performance of the boot to your personal requirements. The most useful is a "stand-and-walk" buckle which releases the forward lean and allows your ankle more freedom of movement when you are walking to the ski lifts for example.

How to choose Comfortable ski boots are an essential (some would say *the* essential) ingredient of an enjoyable skiing trip but they can be hard to find. Sometimes comfort can only be obtained at the expense of performance but this is a compromise well worth making. Fortunately with the latest fitting methods there is no reason to suffer.

The following is a step-by-step guide to choosing boots that will fit and perform well:

1 Always rent or buy from a shop that has experienced sales staff capable of modifying the fit should the need arise. Take advantage of any ski shows since they represent an excellent opportunity to try on a large number of boots (although staff are usually too hectic to provide you with any degree of personal attention).

2 Find out if you can return your boots after skiing should they prove too uncomfortable. This is often known as a "comfort warranty" and allows you a credit towards another pair of boots.

3 Either get your feet measured or check for size by removing the inner boot and standing in the empty shell. If correctly sized your fingers should just slide in behind your heel.

4 Only wear one pair of specialist ski socks. Make sure that the top of the sock reaches above the top of the boot.

5 Always compare several models before making a purchase. Try two at a time — one on each foot.

6 Wear each comfortable boot for 15 minutes and walk around the shop to identify any pressure points.

7 Ask how the fit of the boot can be modified should the need arise. Seamless injection-molded inner boots can usually be shaved or ground down to relieve any pressure points.

8 Check that your heel is firmly held down by pressing your shin hard against the front of the boot and, if this is possible, do this with the boots fitted on skis on the shop floor. The boot should offer reasonable resistance to forward flex. (A forward flex control is a useful feature since it enables you to "tune" the boot according to your weight and strength.)

9 Compare the ease with which you can put on and take off different boots. Rear-entry boots are normally easier to use and walk in.

10 Check the effectiveness of any controls and their ease-of-use by operating them with a glove on.

11 If you have the opportunity, try the boots out on an artificial slope.

Various options are available if you cannot find suitable comfortable "off-the-shelf" boots: the shell can be stretched to accommodate a wider foot; the inner boot can be padded for a narrow foot; and pressure points can be removed by grinding down seamless inner boots. Alternatively, some boots can be custom-foamed, though this is a specialized and expensive service. Some boots can be adjusted for "cant" if you have bow legs or knock knees. And finally, flat feet, or pronation, can often be helped by the fitting of custom-molded insoles.

Sole design 1 Anti-skid toe. **2** *flat area to slide on binding anti-friction pad.* **3** *Cutaway section to reduce weight.* **4** *Anti-skid heel.*

Boot controls *Nordica rear-entry intermediate boot 1. The lower buckle tightens the inner boot with an internal strap and plate. Lange front-entry racing boot 2 with rear adjustment for forward lean angle. Salomon rear-entry intermediate boot 3. The top buckle can be opened to release forward lean for standing and walking. This boot also features a sliding control for forward flex.*

25

SKIS At one time skis were sawed and shaped by hand out of hardwood planks. Wood is still used as a core material for many modern skis but nowadays it is laminated and wrapped (or sandwiched) in complex layers of fiberglass, resins and other synthetic materials.

The all-important base, or sole, consists of a layer of polyethylene which slides very quickly and efficiently over snow. The edges are made of steel and are ground to a right-angle. Up to 15 finishing processes are involved in grinding and waxing a ski base to perfection.

How they work A ski works by sliding, bending and tilting. It has a camber, which means that it curves upward at the center. As you stand on the ski your weight is distributed along the ski so that the full length of the base (apart from the shovel) comes into contact with the snow.

As you press forward and sideways in your boots the ski is steered by its edges. The speed and effectiveness of a ski's steering depend on its "torsional rigidity," the degree of taper from tip to tail, its flexibility and its "sidecut."

A racing ski is torsionally rigid — it has very limited twist characteristics and reacts instantly. A beginner's ski, on the other hand, skids easily and is forgiving of errors because it is "torsionally soft."

A ski's longitudinal flexibility helps determine the snow conditions for which it is best suited. Soft skis are usually preferred in powder snow because they apply less of the skier's weight to the tip, thus enabling the tip to bend upward and "float" above the surface.

Frozen slopes are the most testing conditions for a ski's performance since the ski has to cut across the surface without skidding or vibrating. Reducing the vibra-tion of a ski, without reducing its liveliness or increasing its weight, is a considerable challenge to the ski maker.

Skis only perform at their best if the bases are maintained in perfect condition. The bottoms should be repaired and waxed, and the edges sharpened, on a weekly basis.

How to choose Until you reach a level of technical proficiency where you can tell the difference between various skis, there is really little point in spending a large sum of money on a pair. It is much wiser to spend your money on ski lessons until you reach that level!

If you have decided to buy a pair of skis and are not restricted by any specific requirements it is advisable to economize by buying a "ski and binding" package. Most retailers often offer as much as a 20 percent discount on such a package. Choose a ski recommended by the manufacturer for your ability and take it in a length based on your weight and technical proficiency.

Calculating your ski length The following method for calculating the correct length of ski is based on weight and technical proficiency. Select the appropriate entry for you from each section and add the three points together. Add 100 to this total and this is your ideal ski length (which should be rounded off to the nearest manufacturered length).

This calculation does not take height into account since weight is by far the more important factor in terms of a ski's load-bearing qualities. However, if you are relatively short for your weight (eg 25lb overweight) you may wish to subtract 2-4in from the length you have calculated. If you are over 6ft tall and are thin, you may wish to add 2in to the figure.

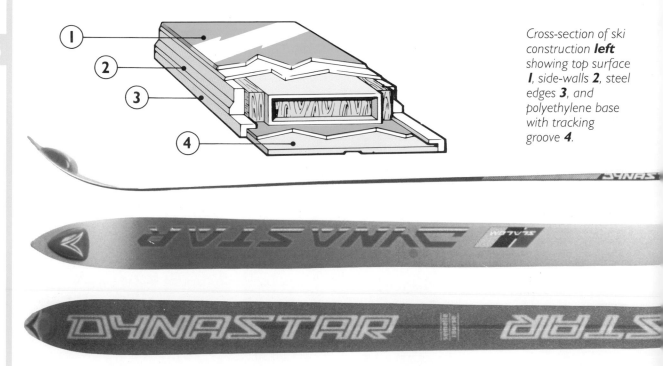

*Cross-section of ski construction **left** showing top surface **1**, side-walls **2**, steel edges **3**, and polyethylene base with tracking groove **4**.*

CALCULATING SKI LENGTH

Points	Your skiing ability
45	You ski to competition standard
42	You ski fast, smoothly and confidently
38	You can now ski mogul fields without traversing
34	You can ski most runs on the mountain
27	You ski at a good controlled pace on medium gradients
22	You ski slowly and carefully
18	You have just learned parallels
14	You are just learning parallels
	Where you like to ski
15	On fast open slopes
13	On all slopes
10	In the moguls or powder
8	On soft slopes at medium gradients
5	On soft slopes at easy gradients
	Your weight
25	Under 66lb
31	66-87lb
38	88-109lb
41	110-131lb
43	132-153lb
44	154-175lb
45	176-196lb
47	197-220lb
50	Over 220lb

(NOTE: Some manufacturers now print length-calculation tables on their skis.)

Ski dynamics *The upward curved camber of the ski **1** evenly distributes the skier's weight. The waisted side-cut **2** helps the ski to carve and steer. The polyethylene base with tracking groove **3** is ground smooth for speed while the groove helps the ski to run straight.*

*The length of the ski **4** determines how fast it will travel — the longer the faster. Most skiers start on skis approximately 1ft shorter than their optimum ski length when technically proficient.*

4

27

1

2

3

SKI BINDINGS At one time a ski binding did exactly what its name implies — it literally bound the boot firmly to the ski. If you fell while wearing such a binding you risked at least a twisted ankle if not a broken leg. Modern ski bindings are, thankfully, far more sophisticated and have greatly reduced the occurrence of such injuries.

The binding itself is essentially a release mechanism — incorporating shock-absorbing springs. It "reads" the level of force acting on the boot (and therefore the leg) and releases the boot from the ski before there is a danger of injury. Thanks to the standardization of boot base design and the introduction of anti-friction devices, bindings now operate very reliably.

How they work Most ski bindings comprise separate toe and heel units which are screwed onto the ski so that the distance between them corresponds to the size of the boot to be worn. Nearly all bindings are the "step-in" type. After locating the boot toe in the cup or "pincer" of the toe-piece, the boot heel is pressed down and locks into the heel-piece.

The springs in the heel- and toe-piece absorb any shocks encountered while skiing. The boot is released when the binding reaches the limit of its elastic travel. The precise force necessary for release is determined by the springs; their stiffness is indicated by a numbered scale and can be adjusted to suit your weight and skiing speed.

In a twisting fall the toe-piece will open; in a forward fall the heel-piece will open. Apart from opening in all types of falls and absorbing shocks in normal skiing, a good binding will minimize friction between the boot and all surfaces it is in contact with. For this reason the anti-friction pad under the boot base is very important.

Some bindings incorporate compensation devices to cope with excessive friction in twisting falls. These feed pressure from the boot into the toe-piece, thus reducing the pressure needed to release the boot from the binding.

An automatic ski brake opens and digs into the snow when the boot is released from the binding. During skiing, when the boot is in place in the binding, the brake arms retract above the ski.

How to choose Virtually all ski bindings are made to conform with the standard DIN (German Industrial Standards Association) boot base, so there should be no problem of compatibility. Your particular choice of binding will depend on your weight and speed of skiing; most bindings are suitable for skiers weighing between 100 and 198lb.

It is a good idea to buy bindings beyond your basic requirements when buying your first pair of skis. When

Binding dynamics *This modern step-in binding with integral ski brake has a toe unit with 'pincer' arms that hold the boot toe. These arms absorb shocks from the boot and open sideways to release the boot in a twisting fall.*
The heel unit closes and the ski brake arms retract above the ski when the boot heel is depressed.
__1__ Toe unit. __2__ Toe height adjustment. __3__ Pincer release mechanism. __4__ Anti-friction pad. __5__ Ski brake pedal. __6__ Ski brake arm. __7__ Heel unit. __8__ Step-in lug. __9__ Exit lever.

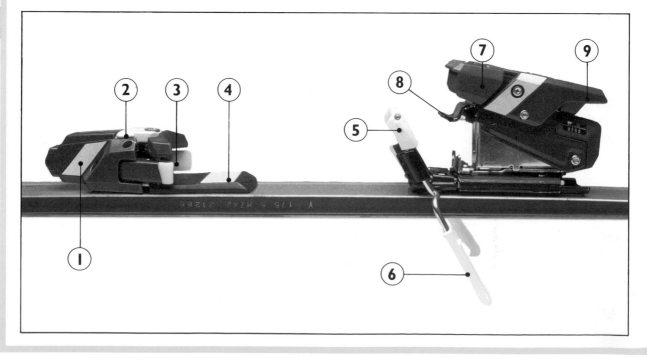

you next change your skis you will then be able to keep the same bindings. If you are tempted by an economical ski "package" which includes a fairly basic binding then consider paying a premium for a superior model (although there is no need to buy the top model unless your weight or standard of skiing justifies the cost, since it will be no safer).

Most bindings are made to pass international tests and there are only minor differences in safety specification between individual models. Some are more convenient to use or have superior shock absorption characteristics, and this is a reasonable basis on which to choose.

Ultimately, a binding is only as good as its adjustment. In some countries the law decrees that skiers are responsible for the correct setting and maintenance of their bindings. All manufacturers publish setting tables for their bindings which should be given by the retailer to the customer. You should always check your binding setting against the relevant table and if the retailer has set them noticeably different, inquire why.

High speed skiing and off-course skiing require a higher setting than normal skiing.

SKI POLES Since ski poles are an aid to the rhythm and timing of your turns, they should be light and easy to swing in the hands. The handles should be easy to grip and should have molded finger positions. A wide base on the handle helps support the hand. Some handles have straps through which you thread your hand, while others have a "sword-like," molded grip.

To check a pole for length, turn it upside down and hold it immediately under the basket. If the pole is the correct length for you, your forearm should then be horizontal.

Ski poles
*These standard ski poles **left** have molded finger positions on the handles and additional supports at the base of the handles to support the hand.*

*To test for length, plant a pole in the snow and choose the one that allows your forearm to lie horizontal **below**.*

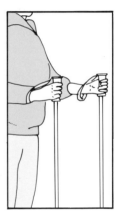

29

Diagonal heel release binding
The heel unit can be closed with little pressure and is opened by lifting the exit lever. The heel can release diagonally in a forward-twisting fall.

Turntable binding *The entire heel unit rotates on a turntable which brings the axis of the binding closer to the natural twisting point of the boot. The heel unit is pressed down for exit.*

Single-pivot toe-piece binding
The toe unit has a curved anti-friction pad which senses additional friction in forward-twisting falls and facilitates sideways release. The toe unit rotates on an "inclined" pivot so that it twists upward to aid release in a backward-twisting fall.

SKI FITNESS

While recreational skiing is not an overly physically demanding sport, it is true that the more inexperienced and technically limited the skier, the more tiring and even exhausting the skiing becomes. Statistics imply that the overall physical fitness of a skier is inversely proportional to the risk of injury — in other words, the fitter the safer. It follows, therefore, that a council of perfection would require any skier, novice or expert, to undergo a specific period of fitness training before setting out on a ski holiday for a week or two. There are two problems with this advice; in the first place hardly anyone will bother to attend special gym classes for this purpose and, in the second, the normal routine at any gym is, oddly enough, totally unsuited to the very specific requirements that ski movements require. Those whose normal lifestyle includes daily jogging, serious walking or cycling will enjoy above average fitness with good muscle tone, while those whose week does not include a visit to a gym or fitness center are most unlikely to subject themselves to the self-discipline of fitness workouts.

BASIC EXERCISES However, it is possible to arrive at a satisfactory compromise with the aid of two, or possibly three, very simple daily "exercises" which will add greatly to your ski fitness. Skiing makes very special demands on otherwise rarely used muscles in the foot,

leg and thigh. The following two exercises will strengthen and condition these very muscles:

*1 — **Knee bends*** Standing flat on both feet, about a shoulder's width apart, lower yourself slowly halfway to the floor, hold this position for a couple of seconds and then, again slowly, straighten your legs. Twenty bends, morning and evening for a couple of months before going skiing, is all that is required.

*2 — **Wall squats*** This exercise, otherwise known as the Killy squat (after the famous French skier), is slightly more strenuous. To perform the exercise you need a non-slip floor, a pair of non-slip shoes and a wall. Stand with your back to the wall and then walk away from it, keeping your back leaning against the wall, until your thighs are parallel to the ground. Hold this position for, to begin with, 10 seconds and then gradually increase this until you can hold it for about 30 seconds without excessive pain.

(An optional third exercise is more concerned with the suppleness of hips and back; it involves no more than hip swivels and circles.)

As a general fitness program, cycling and hill walking are two of the best general activities for strengthening and toning the muscles most used in skiing. However, pre-ski fitness training is just that. It does not give you *carte blanche* to throw yourself around on the slope and it does not preclude the effects of wind and cold on your muscles. It is important to remember that after a cold and long chair-lift or poma ride you should allow yourself a minute or two to warm up and unstiffen legs and shoulders. Most ski schools as a matter of course make their pupils perform a a simple series of exercises before starting off down the slope.

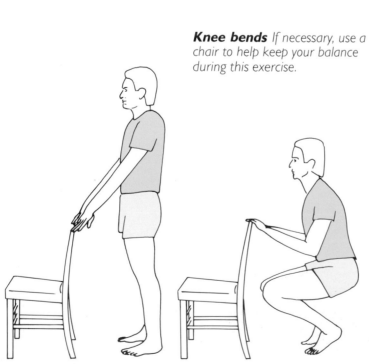

Knee bends *If necessary, use a chair to help keep your balance during this exercise.*

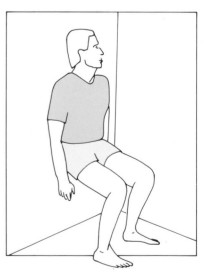

Wall squats *Nearly every skiing technique requires a degree of knee flexing and this exercise is an excellent way of toning up the front of your thighs.*

Warm-up exercises *All ski schools recommend a simple series of warming-up exercises prior to the first run of the day or after a long and cold chair-lift ride.*

Lifting alternate legs

Loosening trunk and waist muscles

Leg and torso stretching

Hip and arm swivels

THE RESORTS

There are about 3,000 ski resorts in the world. They only have one thing in common: they are all located close to mountain territory suitable for skiing, that is to say, they are at an altitude where there is reasonable expectancy of a coherent snow cover for the approximately 100 days of winter. In Europe they lie between 2,600ft and 6,000ft. The tree line in Europe runs at about 5,900ft and the resorts, in general, will be found well below this level, the majority being between 3,600ft and 5,600ft, within the shelter of forest growth and at an altitude which permits some degree of agricultural activity.

The reason is simple. The earliest winter sports resorts, the so-called "first generation," were ancient alpine valley settlements which had, before the advent of skis, been popular summer retreats. The "second generation" of resorts, the great bulk of today's European ski centers, were alpine farming villages which adapted themselves readily to skiing requirements. The "third generation," the purpose-built ski stations, were commercial ventures which involved the building of a catering and engineering infrastructure on bare, uninhabited mountainsides where the mountain geography was ideally suited to skiing.

RESORT STRUCTURE Reduced to its common denominators, any skiing village falls into four regions. The village proper will almost always lie on the floor of a mountain valley giving easy access to the lowland communications and demographic catchment areas. Growing around a central point, nearly always a church, the village may well spread several miles as continual new development of holiday accommodations engulfs former farm land. The fields in the immediate vicinity of the village will usually be almost treeless and, ideally, it is on these gently sloping fields that the so-called nursery slopes for beginners will be located.

The second zone is heavily forested and spreads up, often very steeply, to the upper limit of the tree line at about 5,900ft. Access to this upper zone, the grazing meadows, is by some form of mechanical transportation. Steep paths connect village and grazing meadows and it is often down these paths that skiers find that they must descend to return to their hotel or apartment.

Above the tree line are the real skiing fields, extending up to the level of permanent snow at about 9,200-9,800ft. Here the ground is open, occasionally cut by gullies, with subsidiary summits, rudely called cowhills, adding to the interest and picturesque skyline. It was into this zone that the farmers moved their cattle herds in summer and where the landscape is often dotted with milking sheds, cheese huts and shelters,

*Flaine, France, **above**, is a typical example of a "third generation" purpose-built resort, with a strong bias towards family skiing. It is particularly suitable for novices as the beginner's slopes are incorporated into the central concourse. concourse.*

*St Anton, Austria **right**, was the home of the first modern ski school and is the ultimate goal for most serious skiers. The skiing is difficult to extremely difficult.*

many of which have been taken over to make mountain restaurants.

Above this area are the high-alpine, glacier skiing routes, usually not open until late winter and providing skiing in some areas throughout the summer. Such areas are often served by cable-car, frequently to the actual mountain summits at heights reaching close to the 13,200ft mark.

An exception to this very generalized outline is the created resort where, for a variety of reasons, the resort nucleus is almost invariably located at or just above the tree line, thus giving direct access to the ski fields.

CHOOSING A RESORT The choice of resort is a very personal one. Novices should consider the location and accessibility from the residential area of the beginner's slopes before choosing a particular resort; ideally these should be part of the greater skiing territory but segregated for safety reasons. Many resorts, in order to guarantee adequate snow cover, have placed their beginner's slopes above the tree line; this scenically and socially has many advantages, making meeting with more experienced friends easy and giving the learner a feeling of being part of the skiing scene. It does, however, mean that the return home may well involve taking some form of transportation until skiing skills are

adequate for the home runs. One other thing the novice should look for is a number of easy runs from the higher regions for, within a few days, these will become part of the ski progression. Without being categorical about it, the novice will, generally, be happier in a small resort rather than in one of the prestige centers geared towards the more advanced skier, and with expensive lift passes which the novice can hardly expect to use.

Intermediates are more concerned with the proximity of the daily lifts and the number and variety of the runs which they can reasonably expect to use. As a very rough guide, expect to find more than one run with a maximum vertical drop of not less than 2,600ft.

Expert, advanced skiers hardly need any guidance as to their choice of resort.

There are a number of good ski resort guides available and foremost among these are the freely available tour operator brochures. In addition to these, the national tourist organizations all maintain a good library of literature covering their principal resorts. Two comprehensive guide books are currently available in the British and North American markets — *The Good Skiing Guide* (1985), published by The Consumer's Association and Hodder & Stoughton, and the *Audi Ski Guide*, published annually by Ocean Publications.

The final choice of resort is ultimately down to personal preference and the permutations or combinations of language, nationality, hotel or self-catering, staffed chalet or club hotel, small village or ski town, independent travel or organized group — all have their advantages and detractions. Nevertheless, in the final choice, the familiarity of a name, the possibly subliminal sight of some poster or the casual perusal of a brochure or book will trigger some selection mechanism. And the probability is that it will be weather and new friends and companions which will be the determining factors int he post-vacation inquest.

There are very few outright, bad resorts, but there are possibly some unsuitable ones. St Moritz or Davos may not be ideal for the novice or for very small children as the beginner's slopes are a fair distance away from the residential area and the traffic in the town can be disturbing. That delightful little Austrian village can be a delight to the novice but will quickly frustrate the more advanced skier. Supply and demand has pruned out the impracticable and chronically inefficient and the popular names, the Mayrhofens and Val d'Iseres, have profited from their deserved popularity and have steadily improved their facilities. You cannot go far wrong in your first season if you choose one of the prestige resorts, and once your technique develops there will be no end to the choice.

SKI LIFTS

Chair-lifts are an efficient and sociable means of traveling uphill. Although generally comfortable, a long ride in very cold weather can be something of an ordeal.

Since the earliest days of downhill skiing, the search for a means of taking the skier up a hill to a starting point has occupied eccentrics, scientists, engineers and entrepreneurs. Horses, cows, balloons and wind power have at various times figured in the dreams of these skiing inventors but none proved to be either truly practical or even technically feasible. It was not until the development of electric motors and the internal combustion engine that it was even sensible to consider the problem. Strangely it was not the use of public transportation, such as trains which reached up into skiable altitudes, that were the first to be considered.

EARLY SKI LIFTS The very first patent for a ski lift was taken out in Germany in 1893 by August Goebel. The device enabled people to climb a mountain by means of an endless cable passing over a series of zigzag pulleys to which the climber was attached by means of a rope and a clip. This same patent was later amended to pull a skier in a similar manner. Unfortunately, the electric traction proved to be incapable of handling the load imposed.

Subsequently, various attempts were made to use a rope attached to the jacked-up rear wheels of a Ford motor car. It had limited success in New England but was not altogether satisfactory since it could not operate in the ideal conditions of deep snow, low temperatures and long haulage lengths.

It was left to a Zurich engineer and passionate skier to design the first practical, public ski lift, the now ubiquitous T-bar, which was installed in the winter of 1934-35 in Davos. Erich Konstam gave skiing the missing link necessary to make it a universally acceptable recreational sport, and it marked the real birth of downhill skiing.

LIFT TYPES A resort stands or falls by the quality, quantity and organization of its ski lifts. These can be grouped into two distinct categories: skis off — the gondolas, cable-cars, funiculars and railways; and skis on — the tows (T-bar, Poma and baby-drags) and the chair-lifts.

Gondolas Gondolas are small, egg-shaped vehicles capable of carrying 2, 4 and 6 people, with the skis held in vertical racks on the outside of the vehicle. They travel on a single cable and are stationary when loading or unloading. They present no particular difficulty to the skier and for the operator have the advantage that only the required number need to run, the rest can be parked until needed at the top or bottom station. In Europe, gondolas are limited by law as to the distance

from the ground they can run, but within this limitation they are considerably cheaper to install and maintain than the large cable-cars and, where the ground permits, are increasingly favored as the main up lift, even up to the higher summits.

Cable-cars Cable-cars, originally designed for summer and military traffic to the highest and most inaccessible areas across deep ravines and glaciers, are to be found in most major resorts and can carry anything up to 120 passengers. The main disadvantage with cable-cars is that they are group-loading, and consequently considerable lines build up due to their limited frequency and fixed capacity. Skis are normally carried by the skier inside the cabin.

Funiculars Funiculars, the oldest of the specialized mountain transportation systems, are once again coming back into fashion, being cheaper to install than cable-cars and able to carry larger numbers, and generally unaffected by adverse wind and weather conditions. Several have been constructed as underground railroads. Skis are carried by the skier inside the car.

Mountain railroads are now relatively rare. Some are part of the normal railroad network — the Oberalp/Furka in Andermatt, Switzerland for example; others are specialized mountain railroads originally built for summer traffic but now operating all year round, such as the Wengen/Scheidegg/Grindelwald line, or the Zermatt/Gornergrat railroad. They are fast, convenient and relatively comfortable, but none has solved satisfactorily the carriage of skis, which are usually piled onto an open carriage from where they have to be extricated with the aid of bruised fingers and a most unseemly scrimmage of passengers at the end of the journey.

Ski tows Commonest of all modes of uphill transportation are the various forms of ski tows. The simplest consists of a continuous rope loop with hand-holds at regular intervals. You simply grab a hold and allow yourself to be pulled up the incline. At the top, you release

The platter or Poma lift is efficient and easy to ride.

On beginners slopes the simple rope tow provides an easy means of getting skiers uphill.

Cable-cars are the commonest means of transporting skiers to the highest areas.

the hand-hold and slide away to one side.

The oldest form of ski tow, the T-bar, consists of a continuous cable loop to which are attached, at intervals, a spring-loaded rope-length with a wooden or plastic anchor-shaped purchase. You stand on a designated line and the anchor or T-bar is handed to you from behind or, in the more modern installations, you yourself take it as it passes and pull it down. It is placed at the back of the thighs, half-way between hip and knee; the pole is grasped with the inside hand and the rope is allowed to unroll and tighten. The tow will then slowly accelerate and you should adopt a relaxed position and allow your skis to travel in the grooves formed by other skiers without sitting on or leaning against the T-bar. This device is designed for two skiers, one on each side of the anchor. Many people find this extremely difficult, particularly if there is divergence in height and weight. The key is to be relaxed, with your skis absolutely flat and evenly weighted. Do not lean in or out; leaning in will cause your skis to move outwards and vice-versa.

To dismount, pull yourself forward by the vertical pole and, as you slide away, twist the pole so that the anchor piece is vertical and you can let it go to wind itself up and disappear. Carry your poles in your outer hand and do not let them trail on the snow.

The Poma, invented by a French engineer called Pomagalski, consists of a long pole, flexibly and elastically attached to a continuous cable loop. Unlike the T-bar, it is stationary when you mount it and pulls only one person by means of a small round platter. You enter the starting zone and take one pole in your hand (there is a notice indicating which hand) as high up as possible with your elbow bent, hold your ski poles in the other hand, slip the platter between your legs and, as you slide down a small incline, the pole engages on the cable and starts you off with a jerk. As you start, let the pole slide through your hand to counteract the starting jerk. Just as with the T-bar, do not sit on the platter but let it

pull you. Your skis are guided along the track that has been prepared and do not require any control. On arriving at the top, pull yourself forward so that the platter is free of you and your clothes and let it slide away between your legs as you glide off the lift terminal ramp.

Chair-lifts The chair-lift, carrying from one to six persons at a time, is an American invention. It started life as a banana hoist. Jim Curran, an employee of the Union Pacific Railroad, was appointed engineering manager for their newly conceived ski resort at what is now known as Sun Valley. He decided that skiers were really no different from bananas and adapted his hoist to pick up skiers. Although his invention was adjudged to be too dangerous, he eventually proved his point with the aid of a truck, several bales of hay and some plucky experimental skiers. That was in the winter of 1936. Since that date this form of ski lift is probably the most numerous throughout the world and has been built to accommodate as many as six persons at a time, though the common forms carry three or a maximum of four skiers.

You get yourself ready at a given point in the starting bay immediately after the preceding chair has departed. Holding your poles in the one hand (it is a matter of choice which one, as long as you do not impede your fellow passengers) and, with one hand stretched out behind you, you await the arrival of the chair. As soon as you feel it with your hand, sit down with the chair hitting you, more or less gently, at the back of the knees. If there is a foot rest and safety bar, lower this and relax for a possibly very cold journey to the top. As you approach the top, open the safety bar, lift up the tips of your skis as you cross the entry ramp and then, as soon as the ground reaches your skis, stand up and slide down the ski ramp. Dangerous as it might seem, ignore the chair; it will pass above and beyond you.

35

SKI SLOPES

Ski slopes are the officially marked, prepared and patrolled ski routes under the jurisdiction of either the village community or the lift companies who have acquired lease and transit rights over privately or publicly owned mountain land. Such bodies are recognized in law and have well-defined legal and moral responsibilities. The International Ski Federation (FIS) has established international norms for the classification of these ski highways. North American ski fields have adopted an equivalent, though different standard classification.

The Alps apply four standards (occasionally five in Italy and Spain) — easy, marked in blue; moderate, marked in red; expert, marked in black; and finally, ski routes, unpatrolled and unmarked but indicated by special signposts and frequently shown on ski maps by means of a dotted red or yellow line.

North American ski resorts classify their runs in three categories — easy (round green disks), more difficult (blue squares) and most difficult (black diamond). Certain resorts have an "expert only" category and these trails often have a ski-length limitation as well.

These gradings are relative and are based on average width and steepness. Ideally, these slopes should be uniform in their standard of difficulty, though this is in

*In addition to trail maps, large boards carrying an enlarged copy of the maps can be found actually on the mountain. Here **(above)** an instructor shows her pupils their next run at Jackson Hole, Wyoming.*

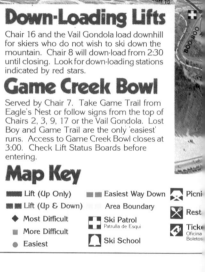

Down-Loading Lifts

Chair 16 and the Vail Gondola load downhill for skiers who do not wish to ski down the mountain. Chair 8 will down-load from 2:30 until closing. Look for down-loading stations indicated by red stars.

Game Creek Bowl

Served by Chair 7. Take Game Trail from Eagle's Nest or follow signs from the top of Chairs 2, 3, 9, 17 or the Vail Gondola. Lost Boy and Game Trail are the only 'easiest' runs. Access to Game Creek Bowl closes at 3:00. Check Lift Status Boards before entering.

Map Key

▬▬ Lift (Up Only)	■■ Easiest Way Down
■■ Lift (Up & Down)	Area Boundary
◆ Most Difficult	✚ Ski Patrol *Patrulla de Esqui*
■ More Difficult	
● Easiest	🔔 Ski School

Picni
Rest
Ticke Oficina Boletos

Trail Information Signs and Symbols on Vail Mountain

North America *There are important differences in trail signs and symbols between Europe and North America. This large board **(above)** in Vail,* *Colorado, displays the three grades of trail as well as one indicating the "easiest way down" (smaller green dot). Other symbols are fairly self-explanatory.*

Europe *In Europe, slopes are graded by color-coded and numbered poles. Blue (easy) runs are usually no steeper than 25 per cent; red (intermediate) runs vary from 25 to 40 per cent; black (difficult) runs are generally 40 per cent or steeper. In addition, most resorts use signs which resemble international road signs to demarcate the slope. Closed-off areas are also demarcated by fluorescent flags strung between orange poles.*

North Side of Vail Mountain

Trail maps All resorts publish a trail map indicating the location of lifts, the name or number of the trail and the degree of difficulty. However, these maps should not be regarded as cartographically accurate. The symbols below provide additional information on the maps.

EUROPE

Blue run: easy

Red run: intermediate

Black run: difficult

NORTH AMERICA

Green run: easiest

Blue run: more difficult

Black run: most difficult

Cable-car

Chair-lift

Drag lift

Funicular

Cross-country trail (loipe)

Toboggan run

Restaurant

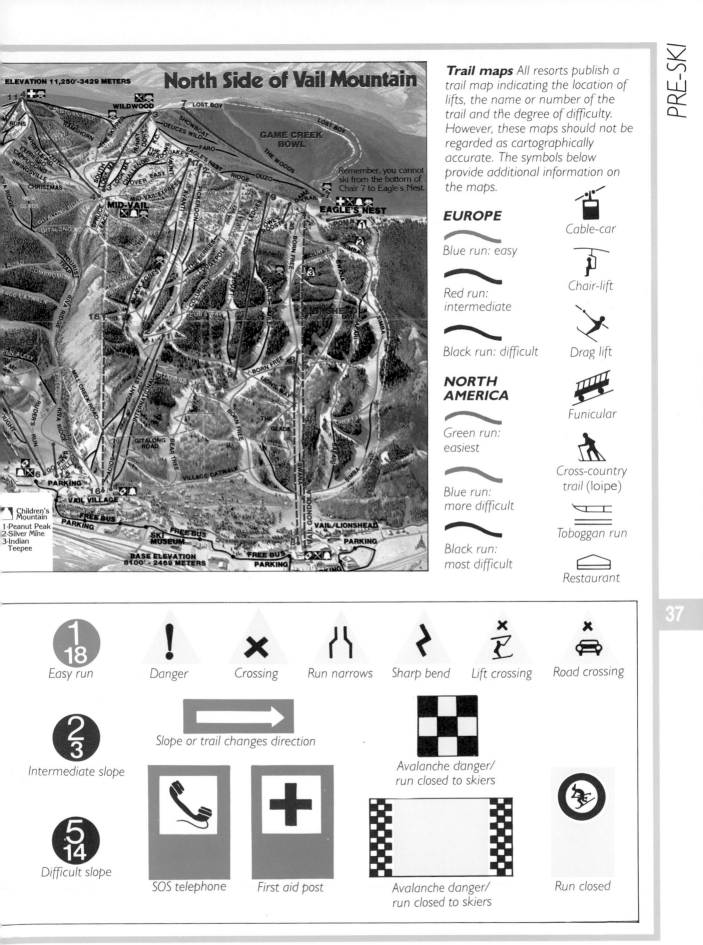

1/18 Easy run

Danger

Crossing

Run narrows

Sharp bend

Lift crossing

Road crossing

Slope or trail changes direction

Avalanche danger/ run closed to skiers

2/3 Intermediate slope

5/14 Difficult slope

SOS telephone

First aid post

Avalanche danger/ run closed to skiers

Run closed

fact rarely the case. It is quite normal to find short, more testing sections, notably in the blue runs, a problem which becomes more acute when snow conditions are varied and difficult. The greatest problems arise in the black classification; many resorts, anxious not to be classed as a "beginner's" resort, will "create" at least one black run which is either mostly unskiable (under the lift cables) or no more testing than an average red run in a big resort. As a general rule, the blues and reds in a small resort will be shorter and easier than those in a major center where length enters into the assessment and the mountain geography is more complex.

SAFETY ON THE SLOPES European resorts are forced, by law, to maintain a fully qualified avalanche protection organization. They are responsible for seeing that the official slopes are rendered safe from avalanches after snowfalls and they are obliged to post special yellow and black avalanche warning signs. Where these are posted it should be taken as a mandatory veto on any skiing in the area or slope designated. Failure to observe this *verbot* renders the skier liable to extremely heavy penalties.

Resorts everywhere are obliged to maintain a ski patrol service. This is usually carried out by the slope maintenance crews who have been specially trained in rescue techniques and first aid. They can be summoned from any lift station (top or bottom) and they also maintain more or less regular patrols. Any skier who finds another skier injured is obliged by convention first to offer assistance and to mark the site by placing the

*All slopes **above** (gradient permitting) are "groomed" by Snowcats. These machines pack new snow into a firm base, flatten out moguls, cover up icy stretches and generally keep the slope in good condition.*

injured person's skis vertically in the snow above him or her in the shape of an "X," and second to summon assistance.

All runs are named and/or numbered and the markers along the slope (lollipop poles) are numbered either from the top or bottom so that the location of a skier along the trail can be identified quickly in the case of an accident. All resorts publish a trail map indicating the location of lifts, the name or number of the run and the degree of difficulty. These maps are not to be taken as cartographically accurate and it is often difficult to reconcile them with a true map. The maps usually show

SKIER'S RESPONSIBILITY CODE

The International Ski Federation (FIS) in Bern drafted its own set of rules at the 1965 Mamaia Congress and these are now the basis in European law for all cases of third party injury. Although perhaps more formally worded, they mirror the skier's Responsibility Code (opposite) and, in addition, expect every skier to observe the following regulations.

1 FALLING ON THE COURSE
In case of a fall, a skier must leave the course free as soon as possible.

2 CLIMBING
A climbing skier must keep to the side of the course and in bad visibility keep off the course entirely. This also applies to a skier who descends on foot.

3 CONDUCT AT ACCIDENTS
At accidents all skiers are duty-bound to assist.

4 IDENTIFICATION
Everybody, witnesses, whether responsible parties or not, present at an accident, must establish their identity.

(Note — The wording may appear to be formal and bland. Litigation has shown that the widest common-sense interpretation should be put on these simple rules. The FIS has published a lengthy commentary on the rules.)

the length and height difference of the various type of lift as well as indicating what kind of lift it is. An intelligent use of these trail maps will give a very good indication of the kind of skiing that can be expected. In addition, by estimating the length of the run against the vertical drop, it is possible to assess the relative steepness of a given slope.

SLOPE MAINTENANCE The slope is nowadays always groomed by what are generically known as Snowcats. These machines not only flatten new snow but also scrape and plow ice stretches and moguls (bumps formed by skiers turning on the same spot). They are, however, limited by gradient and cannot machine stretches which are too steep or narrow. It is on stretches such as these that the challenging and extensive mogul fields will be found. It is also for this reason that you may encounter short, steep passages on an otherwise easy trail which has not been groomed. In addition to the machines, all resorts maintain ski patrols whose duty it is to report any objective dangers such as rocks, deep gullies, tree stumps and the like, to mark them with danger flags and to do manual repair to problem patches as well as to the lift tracks where the constant passage of skiers has produced waves which become extremely difficult to negotiate.

The efficiency and organization of a resort can be judged by the manner in which their ski domain is maintained. It is a very expensive occupation and very time-consuming, particularly since much of the work has to be done at night, when the slopes are clear, and in very adverse weather conditions. The art of snow-farming, as it is called, is of considerable importance to a resort as it is by this means that it is able to maintain skiing conditions until late in the season. Groomed snow does not melt so rapidly, and by grooming immediately after a snowfall and keeping the run closed for awhile it is possible to maintain a skiable terrain when conditions are difficult in the rest of the area.

ARTIFICIAL SNOW Ever since the succession of poor snow levels in the winters of the early 1980s, more and more resorts have installed "snow-makers," an American invention first installed in resorts in New England. These machines, spraying a controlled mixture of water and compressed air at high velocities from a scientifically designed nozzle, produce a very fine spray whose temperature, owing to the sudden compression, is lowered sufficiently to freeze instantly into fine ice crystals. Although the installation is expensive and very noisy to run, it is possible to cover large areas with snow and to ensure that regularly bare stretches are fully skiable. Recently a new development has made this much easier; providing that there is a nearby water supply, the compressor is mounted on a Snowcat and can be moved from site to site, without having to install the complicated air and water lines. The resulting snow, although not quite like the real, sky-born flakes, is still extremely skiable and is proof against all but the most persistent thaw and can be applied whenever the temperature falls below about 32°F.

FIS RULES

There are elements of risk in skiing that common sense and personal awareness can help reduce.

1 CONTROL OF SPEED
Ski under control and in such a manner that you can stop or avoid other skiers or objects. Excessive speed is dangerous.

2 CONTROL OF DIRECTION
When skiing downhill or overtaking another skier, you must avoid the skier below you.

3 STOPPING ON THE SLOPE
You must not stop where you obstruct a trail or are not visible from above.

4 RESPECT FOR OTHERS
When entering a trail or starting downhill, yield to other skiers.

All other skiers shall use devices to prevent runaway skis.

5 RESPECT FOR OTHERS
You shall keep off closed trails and posted areas and observe all posted signs.

This is a partial list. Be safety conscious.

(From the NSAA Classroom Guide for Skier Education published by the National Ski Patrol System, Inc. Reprinted with permission.)

NOVICE

● International Class A & B

● ATM Class A & B

● Austria Class 6 & 5

● France Class Debutant, 1 & 2

● Switzerland Class 1 & 2

The novice skier is as helpless as a new-born infant, confronted with a world where standard values appear no longer to apply. Accustomed by film and television to the grace and speed of skiing, first acquaintance with the cumbersome and bulky equipment comes as something of a shock. The boots appear to be more suited to deep-sea diving; the long, heavy skis and complex bindings by which they are attached to the boots appear to prohibit graceful movement; and then, when you have somehow gathered these together, you are presented with two ski poles with a mind of their own. For many, it is hardly surprising that they are ready to abandon the sport without ever setting foot on a slope.

For those who have the courage to continue, the next stage is to make your way to the ski school meeting place. Here you will meet your fellow "adventurers" and, more importantly, your ski instructor, to whom it may seem you are entrusting your life.

The first lesson will almost certainly take place in a quiet corner of the beginner's area and will consist of a series of ostensibly easy exercises. For many these prove horribly difficult to perform and even the most courageous may begin to wonder if skiing really is something they want to learn.

Thankfully, however, this is a situation for which all ski instructors have been prepared. For the next two days their attention is to make the pupil familiar with skis — how to carry them, put them on, move with them and begin sliding on them. It is called "familiarization." Ideally it is a stage in the learning process which should be taught individually, for no two people will experience the same problems nor require the same corrections; the ski schools are well aware of this but economics make the class system unavoidable. (It is noticeable, however, that North American instructors appear to be more aware of this aspect.)

All ski schools aim, in this first class, to teach the pupil to carry skis safely, put them on, walk, slide on the flat, climb a shallow slope and slide down to the bottom — in fact, to make the pupil feel less like a person with skis and more like a skier. There are very minor differences between the various national schools: only the Swiss school teaches kick-turns at this stage and only this school has a positive section on carrying skis, while all the other schools only instruct the correct wearing of ski poles.

CARRYING SKIS AND POLES

Skis are quite awkward things to carry and, because of their length and the sharpness of the edges, can cause a serious injury if they are mishandled, especially in crowds.

There are essentially two methods for carrying skis (and poles) safely and comfortably — either on your shoulder and balanced by one hand, or held upright in one arm. The skis are held together by sliding them, base to base with the tips upward, so that the ski brakes interlock with the bindings facing outward and the ends of equal length. If necessary, an additional ski strap can be attached around the front ends to stop the skis from sliding about.

If you wish to carry your skis on your shoulder you must make a point of *lifting* them into position rather than *swinging* them, with the tips forward. A hand laid on the skis will then balance them safely, leaving the other hand free to carry the poles, which may also be used as a "walking stick." Alternatively, you can simply carry the skis upright in one hand, tips upward, with the poles in the other. (The latter method is probably the safest in crowds and lines.)

There are basically two ways of carrying skis (and poles). The first, which is probably the safest in crowds and lines, is to hold them upright in one hand, tips upward, with the poles in the other. The second, which is probably the most convenient when walking some distance, is to shoulder the skis with tips forward.

1 *Stand your skis securely in the snow and join your poles together by slipping the tip of one pole through the basket of the other.*

2 *Having joined your poles, plant them in the snow while you get ready to pick up your skis.*

Shouldering skis Having joined and planted your poles securely, grasp your skis and lift them smoothly **2** onto your shoulder, with the tips forward **3**. You should not swing them into position or, turn around without checking that the area behind you is clear of people.

3 Pick up your skis with one hand, gripping them just above the binding or by the toe-piece.

4 Pick up your poles with your free hand.

5 Keeping your skis as upright as is comfortable, you can safely mingle in with a crowd or join a lift line.

43

PUTTING ON SKIS AND POLES

On flat ground, putting on skis is a relatively straightforward process. After separating the skis and laying them down (both pointing in the same direction!) you must then clean the base of your boots of any snow that may have accumulated from your walk across the snow. This is best done by raising one boot in the air and knocking the snow off with your ski pole. The next stage is to kick your toe gently into the front binding and, having previously opened the heel latch, step down into the ski so that the ski brake retracts fully. On sloping ground, the only variation, is importantly, that you always put the lower ski on first.

Wearing ski poles Put the pole strap onto your wrist by sliding your hand into the loop from below **1**, so that when you grasp the pole the strap lies snugly over the top of your wrist and you grasp both pole and strap together **2**. Simply repeat with the other pole.

Having planted both poles a reasonable distance apart, separate your skis and lay one on the snow **1**.

Repeat with the other ski **2**, making sure that both point in the same direction. Raise one boot in the air

3 and knock any snow off the base.

Step into the binding, toe first **4**, and stamp your heel down firmly so that the ski brake fully retracts.

Clean any snow off your other boot **5** and then step into the binding as before **6**, **left**, and then check that both boots are secure.

Putting on skis on a slope *The important point to remember when putting on skis on a slope is always to put the lower ski on first. Stand one ski securely in the snow and use your poles as a balancing aid. Lay the other ski across the slope and edge it in slightly* **1** *to stop it sliding away. Having cleaned your boot base (or asked a friend to help), step across and into the binding as before* **2**. *Standing securely on the one ski* **3**, *place and edge into the slope the other (upper) ski and step into the binding* **4**.

Walking *The whole point of walking on skis is to utilize their sliding potential. Thus you should slide one ski forward and then the other, rather than lifting them into position. In addition, you can use your poles alternately to give yourself an extra push.*

STATIC EXERCISES AND WALKING

To accustom yourself to the weight and balance of your skis a series of simple static exercises is advised. These consist quite simply of lifting and moving the skis from side to side, which helps to show that it is easiest to lift them with your toes. In addition, by leaning forwards and backwards you can sense the degree of support offered by your boots.

1 **Static exercises** Stand square on your skis with one ski pole planted on either side to steady yourself.

2 Using your poles as a balancing aid, lift the tail of one ski so that the tip remains on the snow.

3 Now, lifting with your toes, raise the tip of the ski and bring the whole ski horizontal.

4 Practice bringing the tip of the raised ski across the ski on which you are standing and lower it to the snow.

5 Having taken your poles out of the snow, lean back as far as you can and feel the support offered by your boots.

6 Likewise, lean forward as far as you can and feel the front of your boots holding you up.

SLIDING AND SIDE-STEPPING UPHILL

▮ Sliding *Stand with your knees lightly flexed and your arms forward of your body.*

Having put on your skis correctly and got accustomed to their "feel" and the wearing of the ski poles, you are now ready for your first genuine skiing — sliding. Choose a clear piece of flat ground to being with.

▮ Basic side-stepping *Stand across the slope, holding your upper ski pole well clear of your upper ski. Remember to keep your skis at right angles to the fall line.*

2 *Make the first step by supporting yourself on your lower ski and pole and stepping up with your upper ski. Don't take too large a step and remember to keep your weighted ski edged into the slope.*

2 Plant your poles firmly just in front of your feet and lean forward in readiness for the slide.

3 Push backward with your poles by bending your knees as well as pushing with your arms.

4 Let the poles come free of the snow as you slide forward, arms by your sides.

3 Move your weight onto your upper ski and pole and simply bring your lower ski up in line.

4 Continue the climb by repeating the side-step sequence, keeping both skis edged at all times.

49

CLIMBING TRAVERSE AND HERRINGBONE

The herringbone is a useful alternative for climbing short distances on relatively gentle gradients. It may look ungainly but it is in fact highly effective.

In order to slide down a slope you have first to climb up it. There are essentially two ways of doing this — side-stepping and herringboning. The basic technique for side-stepping is illustrated on the previous page. Many beginners find this quite difficult for no particular reason. Mastery of the basic technique is, however, quite useful since it forms the basis of the climbing traverse — a combination of walking forward and side-stepping. As for the basic side-step, you must edge your skis into the slope while keeping both skis pointing across it, and make a point of taking measured steps while keeping your upper ski pole out of the way.

Side-stepping is the easiest and most efficient way of climbing steep slopes, but for short climbs on gentle gradients the herringbone is a useful alternative. The principle behind the technique is to walk directly uphill with your skis in a broad "V" shape and set on their inside edges so as to prevent yourself sliding backwards down the slope. In addition, by changing your grip on your poles (so that the tip of the grip rests in your palm) you can gain added momentum by "pushing off" from each pole alternately.

3 *With your weight resting on the upper ski, bring up the lower ski either parallel with (for beginners) or in advance of (for experts) the upper ski.*

2 *Now step up the upper ski but this time step it up and forward at the same time, remembering not to take too large a step.*

Climbing traverse *Start from the standard side-step position (see page 48).*

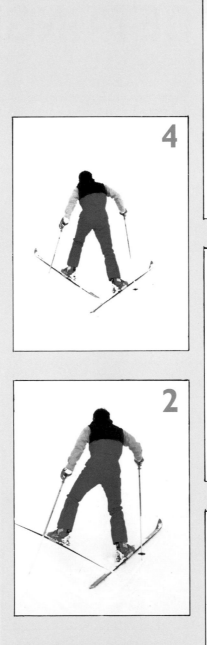

 4 *Continue the climb by stepping alternate skis upward and forward, and try to develop a nice rhythm of vertical and forward steps.*

51

NATIONAL VARIATIONS

 Only herringbone climbing instructed at this stage since novice slope gradients rarely require side-stepping.

 No specific comments at this first crucial stage of instruction.

Herringbone climbing *Place your skis in a broad "V" position, making sure that you keep both ski poles behind your skis so that they provide a platform from which to step up. With your knees angled into the slope (so that both skis are edged), pick up alternate skis, lifting each one up and over the tail of the other, and place them down, edged and back in the "V" position.*

FALLING AND GETTING UP

So far your first steps on skis have hopefully been accomplished safely and you have come to terms with the equipment and environment. However, you will by now have undoubtedly fallen and discovered that getting up again requires its own technique, especially if you have fallen over on a slope, perhaps with your head lying downhill of your skis.

You may think it odd that there should actually be a correct way of falling over since certainly the first few times you fall will be involuntary. However, even an agonizingly slow-motion fall can cause a disabling injury and ruin your trip. If you feel yourself about to fall, the correct and safest method is to sit down to one side and let yourself skid to a halt. You should not put your arms forward to break your fall since this will increase the risk of catching yourself on your ski poles. Keep your arms by your sides with the poles pointing backward, safely out of the way.

Falling *If you feel yourself about to fall, sit down to one side and let yourself skid to a halt. Keep your arms by your sides with your poles pointing backward.*

| Getting up on a slope
Gather your ski poles together in one hand. If you intend to roll over to the right, gather them in your left hand, and vice versa.

2 *Roll over onto your back and raise one ski into the air in preparation for rolling over.*

3 *Lying flat on your back, raise both skis in the air and start to pivot around so that the skis lie downhill of you.*

Getting up on the flat *Gather your poles in one hand and begin to shuffle your skis around until they lie parallel and relatively close together* **1**. *Plant the poles in the snow by your hip* **2** *and, keeping them upright, pull yourself up until you can support yourself on your skis* **3**. *If you find this difficult, try working your way up the poles with one hand while hanging on to the top of the poles with the other* **right**.

4 *As soon as your skis reach a downhill position, lower them to the ground and shift off your back onto your side.*

5 *Raise yourself into a sitting position and shuffle your skis around until they lie at right angle to the slope. With your poles held together, lever yourself upright.*

SLIDING DOWNHILL AND STAR TURNS

Although on an ideal beginner's area it is possible to climb a gentle slope to some flat ground, it is relatively rare that in normal skiing you will always be able to start off from flat ground. You must therefore learn how to turn from a wide-step or herringbone climb into a static position across the slope and then point downhill.

The method commonly employed is called a "star turn." It is performed by stepping around, supported by your ski poles embedded in the snow behind you after climbing in herringbone position, or in front of you on either side after side-stepping. The trick is to take very small steps, first moving the ski which will become the "lower" ski and then the upper ski.

1 Sliding downhill
Face straight down the slope, holding yourself stationary by leaning on both poles (which should be planted in front of you).

2 *To start the slide, relax both arms and flex both knees as if you were about to make a small jump.*

Straight running exercises These simple exercises are intended to build confidence and improve your control of your skis. On a very gentle slope, practice lifting alternate skis without using your poles **1**. *Likewise practice making a series of little hops* **2**, *lifting the ski tails clear of the snow. And finally, practice bending down and straightening up* **3**, *as if you were about to make a standing jump.*

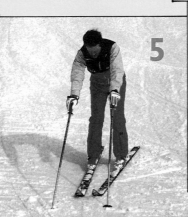

Star turns *Stand across the slope in the normal side-step position **1**. Now plant both poles below you on the slope **2** and start to separate your ski tails. Taking small steps with alternate skis **3** while holding yourself stationary by leaning on your poles **4**, continue to step around until you are facing directly downhill **5**.*

55

3 *As you get underway let both poles pull free of the snow, and adopt a dynamic stance.*

4 *As the slide gains momentum, hold both arms forward of your body with both poles clear of the snow and pointing backward. Your stance should look as though you are about to make a small curtsy.*

THE SNOWPLOW AND SNOWPLOW TURNING

However much the snowplow has been discouraged in the past by many ski schools as indoctrinating an ineradicable and regressive style, common sense has prevailed and it is a ski maneuver which is now a fundamental first step towards ski control. For the novice it is the first indication that a ski's slide down a hill is controllable.

The teaching progression is the same in all countries: the first stage, opening and closing the ski tails on the flat (a difficult exercise whose purpose is simply to give the pupil a feel of the skis in this position and to demonstrate the control offered by the edges) is followed by a gentle slide downhill, opening the ski tails as much as is comfortable and allowing the skis to glide. Hands and legs are kept in the normal running position.

There are two basic plow stances — narrow (known as the "gliding plow") and wide (known as the "braking plow"). In the wide stance, the skis are automatically tipped onto their inside edges, thus braking the slide. If the stance is too wide, however, control over either leg or ski will be lost. Practice is normally confined, therefore, to opening and closing skis during the slide.

Plow turning is nothing more than a shift of weight from both feet onto one foot, while maintaining an equal heel push. The result is to cause the outside (weighted) ski to turn inwards as it is steered by the shape of the inside edge. The steering phase is then terminated by equalizing foot weighting which allows both skis to slide forward in tandem.

Gliding snowplow *The correct gliding snowplow stance: body facing squarely down the fall line, upper body relaxed with arms held out slightly in front of body; poles pointing backwards; and knees and ankles gently flexed.*

Braking snowplow *The correct braking snowplow stance: body facing squarely down the fall line; upper body relaxed with arms held out wide to balance; and knees pushing forward and in to widen "V" shape and force skis onto edges.*

1 ***Practicing the snowplow position*** *Stand in a stationary position, skis parallel and poles planted on either side.*

2 *Start to separate your ski tails by pushing outward with both heels.*

3 *Keep pushing outward with both heels, balancing yourself on your poles and angling both knees in.*

4 *Try not to separate your ski tails too far, since this not only produces a very awkward stance but also makes it very difficult to actually control the skis.*

5 *Start to bring the ski tails back in together again (you may need to lift the tails slightly to achieve this).*

6 *Finish by returning to the original stationary position.*

57

Snowplow turning *From a gliding snowplow* **1**, *increase the weight on the outside ski by flexing that knee.* **2**. *Your weight should be on the front of your foot and you need do no more than let the skis slide and turn* **3**.

NATIONAL VARIATIONS

Snowplow turns not taught. Teaching progresses from very narrow wedge position to heel and hip push (ie swivel) turns practiced with poles but without skis.

Straighten outside leg and apply "turning pressure."

Snowplow gliding and turning only taught in children's classes. Adults taught a narrow snowplow-cum-heel twist turn borrowed from Ski Evolutif method.

Drop outside shoulder and push-turn outside heel. Keep leg positions as for gliding snowplow.

TRAVERSING

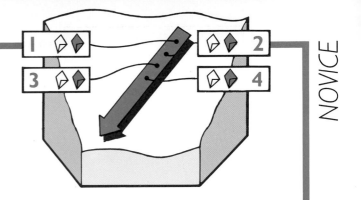

Skiing across a slope (traversing) is a common and useful maneuver. It is in this mode that a ski is most reliably held, by its length and edge, to the slope. The technique is extremely simple.

The skis lie completely horizontal to the slope, held there by their edges. The skier's weight, through the center of the boots, is directly downward. The force acting on skier and skis is a downward gravitational pull, and the more body weight is inclined towards the slope, the more gravity will cause the skis to slide sideways.

The forward movement is, in essence, identical to that of straight running. The one exception (which gives a greater purchase on the slope) is that weight is on the lower ski. In order to achieve this, shoulders are turned slightly away from the slope and the lower, outside, leg is fractionally more bent at the knee. It is mechanically comfortable, because of the slope angle, to have the upper ski slightly ahead of the lower ski, and this is the normal position if the shoulders and upper arm are turned away from the slope and facing slightly downhill.

The overall effect of these seemingly complicated body contortions is to cause a bend at the waist where the knees and thighs are "pushed" uphill and the upper body downhill. It is, however, not an exaggerated position and should feel comfortable and logical.

1 Bring your uphill shoulder forward and flex your lower knee.

3 By holding this position, with the lower ski weighted and shoulders pointing downhill, you will slide forward across the slope.

2 Hold your arms clear of your body and shift weight to the lower ski.

4 Simply maintain this position for as long as you wish the traverse to continue.

NATIONAL VARIATIONS

Taught at beginning-to-turn stage but emphasized as part of side-stepping in Class C.

"Comma" position now dispensed with. Normal "comfortable" stance taught.

Adopt simple, balanced position. "Rounded" side-slipping (ie backwards and forwards with traverse) also taught.

Practice lifting upper ski and stepping uphill. Adopt slight body twist with upper knee and hip into slope.

59

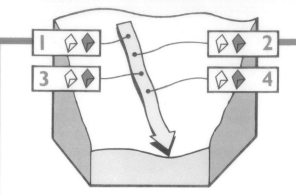

SIDE-SLIPPING

Side-slipping consists of sliding vertically down a slope without, as a rule, any forward motion. It is the single most useful emergency maneuver in skiing, for it enables any skier to negotiate a particularly steep, narrow and difficult passage without at any time losing control.

The technique consists simply of reducing the edge angle of both skis until they start to slide sideways. The skill consists in applying the micro movements of leg, foot and consequently, ski so that the edge angle is decreased precisely the right amount to permit both skis to slide equally downhill. It is easiest on a steep slope; most difficult on a shallow slope.

The body position in a side-slip is the same as that of the traverse (see page 59). The lower ski pole should be held up and behind you so as not to foul your skis. The upper ski pole can be used to prod yourself downward.

From a traverse slide, start the side-slip by relaxing the edge-set of both skis **1**. *Move your knees away from the slope* **2** *and as the side-slip gets going, keep the normal traverse stance* **3** *and use the ski edges to control momentum* **4**. *If anything, weight should be fractionally more on the lower ski.*

NATIONAL VARIATIONS

No great emphasis on perfecting the technique.

'Not taught as distinct maneuver Incorporated with traverse into uphill stop turn.

Turn body into direction of side-slip Distinction made between basic, rounded and linked side-slips.

Push lower ski downhill, slide upper ski after it.

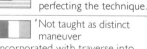

By moving your weight forward and backward, you can alter the direction of the side-slip and negotiate tricky passages.

STEM TURNS

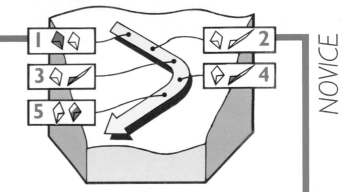

A snowplow turn moves to either side of the fall line (the direct line down any given slope) in a continuous plow or "wedge" position. A stem turn, on the other hand, goes from a traverse in normal traverse position, around, into and across the fall line in a plow position and as the traverse position is again reached, the skis are allowed to close into a normal traverse position, facing the opposite way. The radius of the turn is controllable, as is the degree of sideways skid that terminates the turn, varying from an absolute minimum to a controlled side-slip.

From the traverse position either the upper or the lower ski can be slid into a plow position. The former, upper ski, variation is the most useful and most natural. The "V" position should not be exaggerated since this can lead to a loss of leg control.

When the upper ski is slid, unweighted, into position, the effect is to turn the shoulders and upper body toward the fall line. This ski is then weighted (stood on) and consequently starts to turn. The position is held as you turn through the fall line, keeping your weight forward (on the front of the outside ski) so that as you complete the turn you are once again in the traverse position.

Since the inside ski (formerly the lower ski) is unweighted, it will come to lie parallel to the (new) lower ski. Both skis will tend to skid sideways with the forward turning motion. This is stopped by turning the upper body (shoulders) away from the slope.

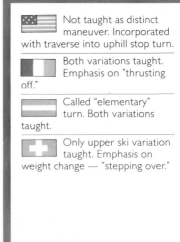

61

NATIONAL VARIATIONS

🇺🇸	Not taught as distinct maneuver. Incorporated with traverse into uphill stop turn.
🏴	Both variations taught. Emphasis on "thrusting off."
⬜	Called "elementary" turn. Both variations taught.
🇨🇭	Only upper ski variation taught. Emphasis on weight change — "stepping over."

*From a normal traverse run **1**, slide your upper ski into position **2**. This will cause your shoulders and upper body to turn into the fall line. Now apply weight pressure to the upper ski **3** and hold this position as the ski turns and you cross the fall line **4**. Keep your weight forward on the front of the turning ski so that you come into the traverse position again **5**.*

HOCKEY STOPS

The hockey stop is far simpler to watch and copy than it is to describe. The technique consists simply of turning both feet in the same direction and keeping the upper body facing downhill. In its simplest form it is merely an exaggerated side-slip.

It can best be practiced by progressing from an uphill stem turn using a lower ski initiation and turning the body toward the slope while pushing downhill with both skis as the turn starts.

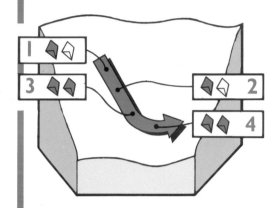

| From a traverse *As you approach your chosen stopping place, straighten both legs in anticipation.*

2 *Turn both feet and begin to flex in the ankles and knees.*

| From a straight run *As you approach your chosen stopping place, straighten up slightly in anticipation.*

2 *Keeping your shoulders pointing down the fall line, gently turn your legs and hips uphill.*

3 As your skis begin to turn uphill, keep both shoulders pointing down the fall line and allow both knees to absorb more of the deceleration.

4 Tip your skis on edge a bit more, and you'll come to an easy, balanced stop.

3 Still keeping both shoulders pointing down the fall line, begin to flex both knees, weight the downhill ski and push both heels downhill.

4 To make a very sharp stop, edge both skis strongly into the slope.

63

INTERMEDIATE

● International
  Class C & D

● ATM Class
  C & D

● Austria Class
  4 & 3

● France Class
  1 & 2

● Switzerland
  Class 3 & 4

An intermediate skier is one who, with comfort and safety, can negotiate any moderate (more difficult in North America) trail or slope. The skills acquired are traverse, side-slip, basic turn (stem or basic swing) and, where possible, the basic or wide-stance parallel turn, while sudden changes of slope gradient or bumps and hollows do not cause instant prostration. The intermediate skier — and that is a category which covers the greatest proportion of all recreational skiers — is no longer a person with skis but a "skier."

To be called an advanced intermediate is an accolade for it implies experience, competence on any kind of snow or slope and a laudable absence of conceit. But in the eyes of the professionals, the advanced intermediate is one who has ceased attending ski school and has spent the succeeding years perfecting errors, albeit with conviction. A brief session with a video can cause such a skier a lasting trauma, emphasizing only too clearly the need for correct technical guidance.

This may well be a technically accurate description of many experienced intermediates but it is grossly unfair and fails singularly to recognize just what recreational skiing is all about. For many recreational skiers the paramount consideration is how much enjoyment they get from their performance and not the accuracy of an objective technical assessment which could fault the best of all skiers most of the time.

The progression from novice to intermediate, in the view of the instructor, consists of the perfecting of skills learned as a novice, and in particular an increase in speed and confidence. The low intermediate is taught to perform more than one turn, to negotiate varied and broken terrain and to link into a continuous run turns, traverses and side-slips. The radius of individual turns becomes increasingly controlled and the basic stem becomes, step by step, the "basic swing" — a term which disguises a practical means of changing direction.

Both Swiss and Austrian ski schools teach elementary stepped turns at this stage. French schools, heading more directly to the basic parallel, do not teach it but, oddly, most French instructors demonstrate it unwittingly. The American method teaches a form of basic swing known as "linked skidded turns" at Class B level.

The end product of the intermediate classes should be the confident performance of smoothly linked parallels with or without stepping, and an ability to ski with pleasure and comfort any moderate run and many of the less horrific difficult runs.

TERMINOLOGY

Skiing has always suffered more than any other sport from a confusion of semantic misunderstandings. This has come about as a result of attempting to express in words the essentially dynamic progressions of a skiing movement. The problem has been greatly exacerbated by having not only to invent or adapt a vocabulary of commands and descriptive instructions, but also to reconcile the eccentricities of Austrian, German and Swiss German and to translate the more academic French terms. Furthermore, the English translations have frequently been inept and misleading, a situation that has not been simplified by the introduction of lay versions of only partially understood psychological learning concepts by some American pundits.

It is inevitable, therefore, that the intermediate pupil will experience some degree of this verbal confusion, and will in turn contribute to it during the course of many *après-ski* discussions of the day's skiing.

The glossary opposite is intended to simplify the problem at this important stage in the learning process, and should be referred to as necessary.

Angulation

Bending

Closed stance

GLOSSARY

Anticipation

Initiation

Open stance

Angulation French description of the sideways flexing of pelvis, thigh and lower leg leading to edge control. Seen from the front, the upper body is angled against the legs.

Anticipation French term describing the preparatory twisting of the upper body into the direction about to be taken by the next turn, rather like winding up a spring. It is used by the American method as a means of upper body turn initiation with pole plant.

Bending (knees, hips, etc) An unfortunate instruction leading to incorrect movement. Flex is more appropriate and more correct. "Bend" to an English-speaker seems to imply a forward bend of the torso. This is not the case in German.

Carving In a pure sense, carving means there is *no* lateral slippage of the skis during the turn. In practice, very few turns actually meet this definition, but modern ski equipment allows top expert skiers to come closer to this elusive goal. Weight commitment to the outside ski, a balanced stance, and applying the right amount of edge are the basic ingredients in a carved turn.

Edge This term refers specifically to the edge of the ski rather than the flat of the base. Edge control is at the heart of all skiing turns and maneuvers. "From edge to edge" means the rapid change of direction from one turn to the next.

Fall line A theoretical line indicating the most direct way down any slope or hill. Every bump or hollow, no matter how tiny, has its own fall line. You can cross it, schuss it, turn down it or fight it.

Initiation This is the term used to refer to the starting of a turn, and it covers the action performed by a skier to make a ski change its direction. Where once this required considerable ski effort, modern skis are so constructed that only the merest hint of "initiation" is required to turn them.

Initiation can consist of unweighting, sliding or stepping a ski into a new direction, weighting the turning ski, edging it or physically twisting or swiveling one or both skis. Any one of these actions or a combination of any or all of them make up the "initiation."

Lower and upper ski The lower is the one further down the fall line, the upper the one closer to the slope uphill. It is customary to talk about the upper ski during the initiation phase of a turn without specifically stating that this ski becomes the lower at the end of the turn.

Open (stance or skis) Definition of the distance between skis or boots. Open implies "with feet apart".

Swing A direct translation from the German *Schwingen*, which in the original implies a rounded, rhythmical turn. The term is now used universally to describe a parallel turning arc.

Thrust A straightening of the knee or knees resulting in a push against the gravitational forces before, during or after a turn.

Unweighting Lessening the weight of both skis by means of a positive body movement either up — up-unweighting, or down — down-unweighting.

Weight Downward pressure on ski. Can be qualified as being forward, in front of the foot or back, on the heel. It can further be defined as being on the outside or inside of the foot. To get your weight forward implies more pressure on the front end of the skis and vice versa.

67

BUMPS AND HOLLOWS

Alpine ski slopes are not universally smooth and flat and the natural waves of the ground, although partially smoothed out by snow and snow grooming machines, are one of the natural, minor hazards of skiing. The skill required to slide over these bumps and hollows without interrupting the smooth flow of your skiing must become instinctive.

The technique consists of maintaining balance while keeping the upper body as still as possible. In other words, you must be a passenger on your skis just as a car driver is a passenger of his car, maintaining control but not directly influencing the bounce of the wheels.

The skier uses his knees, ankles and hips to counteract the ups and downs, exactly like a shock absorber. A hollow must be entered with knees flexed, the whole body inclined forward in front of the static center of gravity which normally passes through the center of the feet. The purpose

The secret of skiing over bumps and hollows is to be able to keep your upper body as still as possible. This involves using your knees, ankles and hips to ride out the changes in terrain and thus act as shock absorbers.

2 *As soon as you cross the apex of the bump begin to let your legs extend down so that your skis remain in contact with the snow.*

1 *As you approach the bump, absorb the rising ground by allowing your knees to ride up while compensating for the deceleration by moving your weight back (yet keeping your upper body as still as possible).*

3 *At the bottom of the hollow your legs should be fully extended, and your weight should have moved forward to be centralized above your feet.*

of this position is to prepare yourself for the increase (however slight) in speed and the altered slope angle. As a general rule, a line drawn through head, hips and feet, as seen from the side, should be at right angles to the slope. As the hollow is descended, the knees are slowly extended so that the upper body attempts to remain at the same height. Hands are usually positioned just in front of the body.

Most hollows are followed by a rise in gradient. This will cause you to slow down while at the same time gravity will push your feet upward (or press your body weight downward — the effect is the same). This must be allowed for by pushing downward with your legs and feet so that this pressure prevents you from collapsing. At the same time, the forward lean should be gradually transformed into a backward lean on the heels to compensate for the deceleration. As you reach the top of the incline, your knees and hips will have absorbed all the differences in gravitational pull and speed and you should reach the top in a normal skiing position.

Failure to compensate in this manner can result in an uncontrolled jump. Since the top of such an incline is a common place for groups to assemble, while you are unable to see what follows such an ascent, you are in considerable danger of either causing a collision or getting into trouble with an unseen hazard.

4 *A succession of bumps should be approached in the same way, and you should try to keep your skis in touch with the snow throughout (even though you may momentarily get airborne).*

6 *Remember to make the correct weight transitions as you climb a bump (weight back to counter the deceleration) and descend a hollow (weight forward to counter the acceleration).*

69

5 *Try to get into a rhythm of flexing on the bump and extending in the hollow.*

TRAVERSE, SIDE-SLIP AND UPHILL STOP

The commonest route is across the fall line — a traverse. Irrespective of whether this is shallow and slow or steep and fast, it is the slide which connects, however briefly, two turns. It is also a ski's strongest and safest means of crossing steep slopes, as the length of the ski gives a far surer purchase on the snow than a ski boot can.

The basic traverse position is traditionally part of the novice instruction, and now that the various national ski schools have abandoned some of the more extreme, exaggerated and unnecessary stances, there is virtually no difference to be detected. Weight is largely on the lower ski, shoulders are turned slightly downhill, upper arm and ski pole are advanced to just in front of the foot and the weight is evenly distributed over the whole sole of the foot. The upper ski is slightly in advance of the lower, both for comfort and as a result of the twist given to the shoulders. The traverse position is nothing more than a reasonably prepared stance to stand comfortably across the angle of the slope, facing the way you intend to go — that is across and down — and from which you can instantly turn uphill and stop, start a turn across the fall line or start a side-slip.

A traverse is nearly always accompanied by a controlled slide-slip, more accurately described as a side-slide, for it is a controlled and directed movement. The purpose of the traverse side-slide is to lose height at the same time as moving forward. The initiation of the side-slide is carried out by a

The traverse, traverse side-slip and uphill stop are closely associated maneuvers, and even if an uphill stop is not required, the body positions for turning out of the side-slip position are similar to those for the initiation of the turn.

7 *As the uphill turn comes to a stop, allow both knees to flex and set your skis on an acute edge.*

6 *To bring the uphill turn into a stop, simply apply more weight pressure to both skis by flexing your knees (but still keeping both shoulders pointing downhill).*

5 *As the skis start to turn uphill turn your shoulders so that they remain pointing downhill.*

down unweighting accompanied by a very moderate downward heel push which turns the ski tips across the slope. In other words, knees are flexed, the heel push originates at the hips and is transmitted through thigh and leg, and the foot weighting is moved to the center of the skis. At the same time the edge-grip of the skis is relaxed sufficiently to permit the skis to slide sideways.

Although this reads as a very intricate combination of demands it is, like all ski movements, only involved if analyzed in detailed, step-by-step action. In practical terms, however, and viewed as a skill rather than a technique, the entire sequence and combination is the result of a single positive action — the relaxation of edge control. For this to result in a controlled slide as opposed to a "slip," it is necessary to counter the instinctive reactions. The heel push, weighting change and shoulder rotation are all designed so as to result in a controlled, deliberate sideways slide. As the skill is acquired, so all these individual actions become fused into one single action.

This position is held as long as the side-slide is required; it can be exagger-

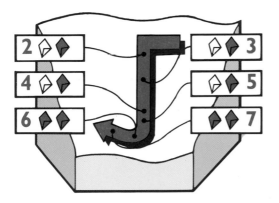

I *From a normal traverse position, reduce the amount of edge on the lower ski and with a down unweighting initiate the side-slip.*

4 *To turn the traverse side-slip into an uphill turn simply push both heels downhill.*

3 *Control the speed of the traverse side-slip by increasing or decreasing the amount of edge-set.*

2 *Move foot weighting to the center of the skis, lift your upper arm clear and point your shoulders in the direction in which your skis are traveling.*

ated by increasing the flex and heel push and decreasing the edge-set, and can be terminated by resuming the normal traverse position and increasing the edge-set.

To turn the traverse side-slide into an uphill stop, the side-slide initiation is increased until the skis come to a stop. It is important that the shoulders are kept facing downhill (sometimes called "counter-rotation" — body rotation in the opposite direction to that of the turn). If the body is turned into the slope, the skis will turn too far, the tails will come to point downhill and you will slide backward and most probably fall.

All ski schools teach this form of stop turn (called a "hockey stop" in North America) and all illustrate it with greatly increased knee flex. A common mistake is to allow weight to move to the upper ski, which has the effect of causing the ski to catch and turn rapidly uphill.

The technique for performing this kind of stop turn is exactly the same on flat or sloping ground, and is the commonest kind of stopping maneuver after any downhill slide. However, it should be pointed out that it is the height of bad manners and a breach of ski safety to shower a fellow skier with snow when stopping in this manner. Wherever possible, the stop should be carried out *below* other skiers so that should you encounter a patch of ice or momentarily lose control, your resulting fall will not sweep other skiers down the hill with you.

The aim of this skill is to enable you to cross a relatively long slope of varying gradient with a controlled combination of traverse and side-slide at a chosen speed.

Overturning from uphill stop *A common error made when performing an uphill stop is to "overturn." This comes about if you allow your shoulders to follow the direction of the turn/stop instead of keeping them facing downhill throughout the maneuver. The result of overturning is the alarming one of finding yourself sliding backward down the slope out of control.*

The problem is essentially one of rotation. Your shoulders must be kept facing downhill (ie counter-rotated against the direction of the turn) while your legs are allowed to rotate with the turn. Any failure to balance out the rotation and counter-rotation will make the uphill stop very difficult to perform.

STEM TURN OR BASIC SWING

It is fashionable today to equate stem turns with novice skiers. Not only is this wrong in fact but it also displays an ignorance of the importance of the stemmed (as opposed to snowplow) turn in everyday skiing. It was for this reason that some 10 years ago it was agreed internationally to name this turn and all its many variations the "basic turn" or "basic swing" — for that is exactly what it is. The term "swing" is now incorporated into the official Austrian instruction language, implying a roundness and dynamic rotation as well as smoothness.

The stem turn consists of an initiation by means of "stemming" out one ski from the traverse, closing the other ski up to the turning ski at some optional point in the turn and completing the turn facing in the opposite traverse direction.

The basic swing or turn can use a broad or narrow stem phase, and it can be closed before, in and after the fall line. It can also be slid or stepped. In all its versions, the turning impetus derives in the first place from displacing one ski into a new direction, and secondly by an unweighting movement which frees the tails of the skis sufficiently to react to a turning force. The turning force may be directly applied by means of a twist (or heel push) or it may be the result of some other body movement transmitted through some form of leg and foot action.

The initial stemming movement can be performed by the upper ski or the lower ski. These variations give two distinct forms to the basic or stem turn and each has its appointed place. It is a matter of opinion which should be taught first.

THE UP-STEM Stemming the uphill ski is generally accepted as being the easier to learn. Since the turn is started from the traverse position, the uphill ski is relatively unweighted and consequently can easily be slid up into an "A" position. Once in this position, weighted pressure is applied either as in the case of the snowplow by sinking a shoulder or knee, or, more correctly, by pushing or thrusting upwards from the lower, weighted ski. The resulting shift of stance enables a turning movement to be made by the legs. The weighting is held on the turning ski and, as you pass into the fall line, the now unweighted lower ski is turned to join the steering ski. A skidding turn will have been started which is held until the new traverse position is reached. The turn is stopped just as a traverse side-slip is stopped. In practice, the up-stem is most useful on steep ground as it gives constant and sure control of the turn without relaxing the edge-hold of the lower ski.

To close the stem after passing the fall line nothing need be done except to allow the upper, unweighted ski to slide forward and parallel with the lower ski, which it will do without any assistance. To close the stem in or just before the fall line, both feet are straightened (or both feet are thrust downwards) which results in an up unweighting and permits both skis to skid around into the turn. As both skis come parallel with each other (which happens automatically) both knees are flexed and the weight on the lower foot is transferred to the front of the foot, pushing the inside ski forward.

Failure to transfer weight in this manner results in the skis shooting forward and rotating too far or "scissoring." It is a common mistake among low intermediates (often confined to turns in one direction only) that can be cured very simply by the instructions to "stand on your lower big toe," a feat impossible to perform — even in a token fashion — without moving your weight to the front of the lower, outside foot and ski.

THE DOWN-STEM More elegant is the basic turn or swing which is started by stemming out with the lower ski. The effect of this single movement is to produce a braking action (which may be very welcome) and to give you a platform from which to start the turn.

Stemming the lower ski will, for an instant, check your progress across the slope; you then thrust upward with the stemmed ski, bringing the weight forward by means of the thrust. Since this thrust will induce a turning action to the upper ski, and also because the thrust is an upward movement, it will unweight both skis for an instant and they will start to turn. Technically speaking, this chain of instructions introduces an error since the lower ski will be on an outside edge while the upper ski will be forced onto an outer edge if the stem is too broad. In practice, however, this is not really the case since the almost instantaneous weight transfer upward automatically corrects the edge-set.

Viewed as a rhythmic sequence of movements, the turn can be analyzed into this progression; stem out — body down — body up — skis together — body down. It is the classic down-up-down weighting sequence which is produced by nothing more than stepping from one ski to the other.

Stem technique The stem turn (or basic swing) moves from the traverse position across the fall line and back into the traverse position again. Stem out your uphill ski **3**, **4**, weight it **5**, allow the turn to develop and as you cross the fall line bring your skis together by straightening both knees **6** and moving your weight onto the (new) lower ski **7**.

The up-stem variant is the commonest form of stem turn initiation not least because it is compatible with nearly every situation. For this reason it is the variant most widely taught in all ski schools.

The down-stem variant is, however, particularly useful on steep slopes and where a braking phase is felt to be necessary. It has the advantage over the up-stem initiation in that it produces through the momentary braking phase a kind of platform from which it is easy to thrust upward.

1 ***Up-stem*** *Coming out of the traverse position, begin to stem out your upper ski and slide it into an "A" position.*

2 *With the upper ski now in position, apply weight pressure by pushing or thrusting upward from your lower, weighted ski. The resulting shift of stance enables you to make a turning movement with your legs.*

3 *Hold your weighting on the steering ski and, as you pass into the fall line, bring the now unweighted lower ski around to join it.*

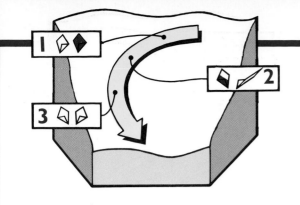

Down-stem
Coming out of the traverse position, begin to stem out your lower ski. This will produce a slight braking action and provide you with a platform from which to start the turn.

2 Now thrust upward from the stemmed ski and bring your weight up, forward and against your uphill ski. This will induce a turning action to the uphill ski.

3 As you pass into the fall line, bring your skis together and complete the down-up-down weighting sequence by sinking back into the traverse position.

TURN AND TRAVERSE RUNS

Skiing does not consist just of a single turn or a single traverse, but rather it is a combination of a linked series of traverses and turns covering what might be called a "stage." These stages are not haphazard but are carefully planned by the ski instructor, who is trained to lead his class according to their ability and to the nature of the terrain.

An instructor will always start from a safe point which is as flat as the ground will permit, and will continue to another such place which is in clear view of all the class. He will not start a fresh stage until the last member of the class has arrived and has had a chance to rest and get ready.

To really enjoy skiing a stage it is necessary to think in terms of a rhythm — traverse, turn, traverse, turn and so on. This rhythm prepares you for the next traverse or the next turn, since the body position resulting from the one is the preparation for the other. This is also the result of thinking ahead and feeling your turns and traverses rather than thinking solely in terms of a single element of the sequence.

It is extremely difficult to perform a single turn in isolation and this is the one demonstration all instructors fear in their examinations. Likewise it is not always possible, because of a lack of rhythm, to perform the first traverse and turn of a stage as well as the middle sequence.

Choose the place for each turn a whole traverse in advance and try to turn exactly where the instructor turned; it was not a chance turn that he made but was placed so that it will not only lead to the correct, following traverse, but will also be the easiest place for the turn to be carried out.

1 *Ideally you should start the turn and traverse run sequence from the traverse position (see page 59). Look ahead and try to choose the exact location for your turn.*

5 *Initiate your next turn with an up-stem, and induce the turning movement by weighting the stemmed (steering) ski.*

6 *For this turn keep the stem position through the fall line with both legs extended.*

2 As you approach your turning spot, initiate the turn with an up-stem (see page 76) and pass into the fall line.

3 Close the turn in the fall line by thrusting both feet downward to produce an up unweighting which will permit both skis to skid round into the turn.

4 As you come out of the fall line, with both skis parallel and both knees flexed, settle back into the traverse position and look ahead to plan your next turn.

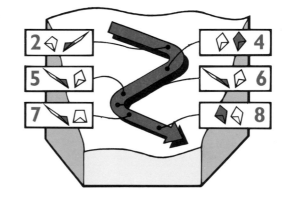

7 Close the stem after the fall line by allowing the upper, unweighted, ski to slide forward and parallel with the lower ski.

8 Settle back into the traverse position, with shoulders turned to face down the slope.

9 Finish the sequence by running free and straight, with shoulders facing the direction in which you are traveling.

USING SKI POLES

Ski poles have three distinct functions: they are a support and walking aid; they help overall balance in much the same way as a tightrope-walker's pole; and most important of all, they serve as a turning fulcrum or support which at the same time stabilizes the upper body for a turn. The importance attached to this last function by the various ski schools varies greatly, but rarely exceeds the very general statement that to plant the ski pole correctly on the inside of the turn will help you to carry out a turn.

To start the pole plant, tilt your hand/wrist forward to keep your elbow clear of your body. Point the pole down toward the chosen place, stretching slightly forward and turning your body to locate it correctly. The location of the pole plant is, theoretically, at the center of a semicircle, which will be defined by the turn that is to follow. But in practice, however, since most turns are ovoid rather than semicircular, the aim is to plant the pole more or less opposite the apex. It is, in fact, immaterial whether the point is actually sunk into the snow or just brushed onto the surface. The higher the speed of the maneuver the less time there is to actually plant the pole, and the technique requires more of a "prod" than a "plant."

The importance of the pole plant is three-fold: firstly it locates the turn (and makes you think about where you are going to turn); secondly it provides the timing of the downward unweighting; and thirdly, and most important of all, it gives support to the upper body as it twists (rather like winding up a spring) against the forward motion of the skis. The moment the friction of skis on the snow is reduced, the skis (and your feet, legs and hips) rotate to bring your body into line. This alone is sufficient to initiate the turn without any further twisting of the feet. It is the basic movement of "anticipation" and is fundamental to turn initiation in that it obviates every other theoretical consideration apart from unweighting.

Ski poles serve three important functions — as a support, as a balancing aid and as a turning fulcrum. Their correct use is crucial to the development of a sound technique, and they must be seen as active components of technique and not mere appendages.

1 ***The pole plant*** *Approach your chosen turn location with arms by your side and slightly forward of your body. Weight should be central on both skis.*

2 *To start the pole plant, tilt your wrist outward and move your elbow clear of your body in anticipation of the plant.*

3 *Lead in to the actual pole plant by targeting the pole at the precise point around which you want to turn and lowering your body.*

NATIONAL VARIATIONS

Stressed as essential part of turn timing and placement.

Emphasis on (theoretically) correct location of plant.

Stressed as essential part of turn initiation. Action used as part of down unweighting movement.

Emphasis on timing and placement.

4 As you plant the pole note the support it gives to your upper body as you twist against the forward motion of the skis and rise in anticipation of the turn.

USING THE TERRAIN TO ASSIST TURNING

As anyone who has practiced on an artificial slope will know, turning on absolutely even ground is difficult. Luckily, however, no real snow surface is completely flat and a pair of skis passing over it are rarely in contact with the snow along their whole length.

An interesting way to demonstrate the turning assistance offered by variations in the terrain is to stand on the peak of a small bump so that the tails and tips of your skis are well clear of the ground. The slightest body movement will rapidly demonstrate how easily the tips and tails move about and the skis will tend to wander forward and backward.

The demonstration can be taken a stage further by performing what amounts to a stationary turn. Choose a small bump with a nicely rounded peak and stand so

that you are well balanced with the tails of your skis touching the snow when you lean back a little. Plant your ski pole in front and to one side as if you were about to turn around the bump, and then bring your weight forward so that the ski tails are free of the snow. As soon as you do this you will find that both skis swivel around to point in a new direction as you slide off the peak of the bump — executing, in essence, a stationary turn.

To put this theory into practice, slide slowly toward a suitably small bump. Using a down-stem and pole plant just beyond and to one side of the bump, note how easily your skis turn as they cross the apex of the bump. It is for this reason that you should always try to use any slight unevenness in the snow surface to locate your turns.

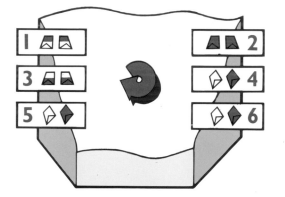

6 The turn over, move on in the normal traverse position.

5 Complete the turn by counter-rotating shoulders downhill while bringing your arms into line.

4 As the skis pivot and slide off the crest, transfer weight to the new lower ski.

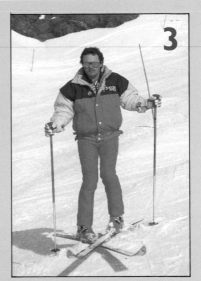

How the terrain helps To demonstrate how maneuvrable skis become when they straddle any variations in the snow surface, stand on top of a small bump so that both tips and tails are clear of the ground **1**. Note how easy it is to make the tips diverge **2** and converge **3** simply by exerting minimal turning pressure. However, this apparent advantage does have its drawbacks since it also demonstrates how difficult it is to make both skis react in the same way and thus act in tandem.

I **Stationary turn** Stand stationary on a small bump so that the tips of your skis are clear of the snow and the tails rest on the snow when you lean back a little.

2 With the inside ski pole planted forward and to one side, rotate your shoulders into the direction of the intended turn.

3 To induce the turn, simply bring your weight forward and use the rotational tension caused by turning your shoulders.

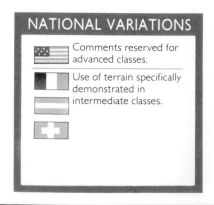

2 Absorb the rising ground and time your up unweighting so that you are fully flexed on the bump's apex and your shoulders are partially rotated into the direction of the turn.

1 ***Using the terrain*** *Having practiced the stationary turn (see page 83) repeat the exercise in motion. Approach a suitable small bump, use a down-stem initiation and pole plant just beyond and to one side of the bump's apex.*

NATIONAL VARIATIONS

Comments reserved for advanced classes.

Use of terrain specifically demonstrated in intermediate classes.

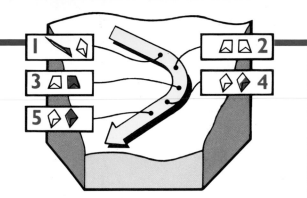

3 Since only a small portion of the skis are in contact with the snow at the apex of the bump, it's easy to turn your legs in the direction you want to go. (Notice the solid pole plant which helps provide better balance.)

4 With the turn virtually completed, extend both legs to compensate for the drop into the hollow behind the bump, and prepare to move your weight back onto the lower ski.

5 As soon as you are clear of one bump you must get ready for the next. Flex both knees, turn your shoulders to point downhill and look ahead for a suitable bump.

85

STEPPED TURNS

A step turn consists of stepping from the weighted ski to the unweighted ski in a normal stepping motion while lifting the unweighted ski into a new direction. This ski is then weighted and, with the aid of a pole plant, starts to turn.

A turn is said to be "stepped" when, in the initiation phase, the upper or lower ski is stepped (lifted) into a new direction, weighted and then turned. Stepped turns are not a new innovation and indeed were practiced as long ago as the 1920s, when they were known as "lifted stems." However, the technique fell into disuse largely because it tended to cause imbalance, and it was superseded by the safer and more elegant "slid" stem.

Recently, however, the spectacular career of Ingemar Stenmark (the world-famous slalom racer) has returned the technique to favor. His rhythmically elegant giant slalom style, stepping apparently effortlessly from one edge to the other and carving the resulting turn, has focused attention on the benefits of the technique and has highlighted the way it provides an instant edge change to the steering ski. Strictly speaking, stepped turns could be divided into three categories — step-up, step-down and "scissors." In practice, however, the intermediate skier need only be concerned with the variations possible on the theme of "step-up" turns.

In essence a step turn consists of nothing more complicated than stepping from the weighted ski (normally the lower) to the upper, unweighted ski by thrusting upward in a normal walking or stepping motion from the lower ski, lifting the upper ski clear of the snow and placing it in a new position or direction. At the same time, the inner ski pole is planted in the center of the radius of the new turn so that an "anticipatory" rotation of the upper body is produced. When the upper ski is stood on (weighted) it receives a turning impetus from this combined movement and commences to turn. The lower ski is then stepped up and forward parallel with the turning ski and the turn is completed in the normal manner.

The stepped ski can be placed in a stem position or parallel to the lower ski. The end effect is the same, though the former is easier and gives greater confidence. The one can transform into the other almost imperceptibly and it would be a foolish skier who thinks he always parallel-steps.

The actual step must be a positive movement and the actual stepping motion an up and forward thrust. A useful way to practice the elements of the technique is by stepping over a ski pole or line of poles laid on the snow (see page 89). The subsequent weighting or pressure change must be equally decisive and the inside edge should bite immediately.

The body movements involved are traverse position (see page 59), down, thrust up, and down during the last phase of the turn so that you are ready for the next turn. Legs and feet turn under the body while the upper body automatically twists against the rotation of the turn as you prepare for the subsequent one.

Experience shows that the step-up variation is the most versatile turn of all for intermediate skiers, a development which is already evident as skis become increasingly easy to steer.

The key point to bear in mind is that the step itself should be as natural and smooth as stepping over a stone on a country walk; it should be the product of balance skills and a demonstration of the independence of the two skis. Only two movements are of importance — the step-up thrust and the pole plant. Everything else should be an inevitable consequence of these two actions which are virtually simultaneous.

However, you must become tuned in to a dynamic change of direction — instant stepping over onto the edge means instant turning. To maintain your stability during the turn you must automatically change your angulation through the stepping action.

Given the skill of independent leg/ski action and the experience of successful turns across the fall line in a stem progression, the performance of a stepped turn should prove to be extremely simple and one that can be performed in virtually any situation.

1 Approach the planned location of your stepped turn in the normal traverse position, with both knees lightly flexed in preparation for the turn.

2 Lift and step-up the upper ski by thrusting upward from the lower (weighted) ski in a stepping motion, and begin to turn your shoulders into the new turn direction.

3 Place the stepped-up ski into the new steering position, apply weight pressure and bring the lower ski up and parallel with the steering ski.

4 It is quite usual for the lower ski to be kept in the air until the steering ski has turned through the fall line.

87

5 Step the raised ski down parallel with the steering ski to finish the turn.

Step turning on steep slopes

Make an anticipatory pole plant, flex both knees and step your upper ski in the direction of the turn **1**. Weight this ski and let it steer the turn while smoothly lifting your lower ski up and around to lie parallel with the steering ski **2**. Keep your weight well forward on the (new) lower ski **3**, and follow the turn through until you can move back into the traverse position.

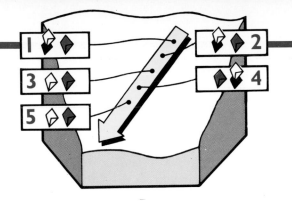

Practicing stepped turns The best way to practice step turns is to lay a line of ski poles on the snow to demarcate the location of each turn and over which the turn must be stepped.

As you approach the first pole, raise your upper ski **1** so that it is over and across the marker pole by the time your lower ski is level with it **2**. Now lower the raised ski into the new steering position **3** and get ready to raise your other ski to step over the second marker pole **4**. Step over and across the second marker pole and lower the raised ski to the ground into the new steering position **5**.

NATIONAL VARIATIONS

Not taught in intermediate classes (but introduced later). Proceeds directly to wide-stance parallels.

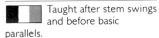

Taught after stem swings and before basic parallels.

Only taught in advanced competition classes

Taught as further development of basic parallel.

ROTATION

The term "rotation" is one that is continuously used to define body position before, during and after a turn. It is also a term that causes considerable confusion for pupils who attempt to respond to instructions to rotate their knees (an anatomical impossibility), to rotate their shoulders (an impossibility without turning the whole trunk), to not rotate, to rotate more or to counter-rotate.

So what exactly is "rotation" and "counter-rotation"? Quite simply it is the turning of the whole body, led by the arms, shoulders and trunk, which is transmitted to the legs when a change of direction is started, carried out and terminated.

Stage one is always rotation. The body is turned into the direction about to be taken and gives the turning movement, the initiation, to legs and skis. As you turn, there is an instinctive tendency to continue rotating with the turn. This is a very common fault and has the effect of causing the skis to continue turning beyond the point when you want to re-assume the traverse position.

Stage two, therefore, is always counter-rotation, which not only stops the turn but also forms the preparation for the next turn.

Taken as an isolated, single turn, this would seem to be illogical. However, one turn is normally the precursor to the next and the preparation for that turn is, in effect, a counter-rotation of the body as it stops the previous turning motion. In any event, prolonged rotation will always result in over-turning and is a common fault when skiing slowly and planning only one turn at a time. It is also a common error caused by a failure to use pole planting as the pointer to a turn and allowing the arms to swing in an uncontrolled fashion, probably attempting to balance out the turning motion of the swing just completed.

Although rotation/counter-rotation is the normal progression, it is not sacrosanct and there are variations of parallel turns which require counter-rotation in the initiation phase.

In skiing practice, it is the arms and ski poles which determine and control the rotational movement of the body. It would be more logical (and easier for learners to understand) for the instruction to "rotate" to be replaced by the instruction to "bring your (outer/inner/right/left) ski pole forward or back."

4 *With your shoulders fully rotated into the turn, the twisting tension is transmitted through your hips and legs to make the skis turn.*

5 *As you pass through the central phase of the turn, your skis respond to the turning force and come to align with your shoulders.*

I *Approach your chosen turn location in a straight run, with shoulders pointing in the direction in which you are traveling.*

3 *Plant the pole at the point around which you wish to turn. This will impart a full rotation to your shoulders so that they now point into the direction of the turn.*

2 *Commence the first stage of the turn by bringing your inner arm forward in anticipation of the pole plant. This will impart a slight rotation to your shoulders.*

6 *With shoulders and skis now pointing in the same direction the turn is completed and you must now get ready to counter-rotate to prevent the tendency to overturn.*

7 *Counter-rotate your shoulders against the turning momentum so that your shoulders are once again pointing downhill.*

8 *Having counter-rotated against the turning momentum you are now ready for the next turn.*

BASIC PARALLEL TURNS

The basic parallel turn is the foundation of a whole series of advanced turns, and represents a crucial stage in the learning process for it confronts the pupil with the problem of getting both skis to turn through the fall line.

The ultimate skill which every novice skier hopes for is to be able to perform parallel turns. Viewed quite objectively, however, it confers no particular advantage beyond style and, possibly, an increase in speed and slope control, though the latter is more of a subjective impression than a physical fact. For the less athletic and the older age groups, parallel turning requires greater physical effort, balance and reflex sense, leads to a more uncontrolled style of skiing and involves a great deal more instruction and practice than is necessary to reach an equivalent level of ski control by means of minimal up-stem basic turns and step-up basics.

The parallel turn is a totally different kind of move from all that has gone before, though a hint of the ski action involved is contained in side-slipping (see page 60) and stop turning (see page 62). Where all the forms of stemmed turns depend to some extent on one ski being *steered* into a new direction, the parallel turn involves unweighting *both* skis, initiating the turn with *both* skis and changing edges on *both* skis. This may seem self-evident, but what is often not realized is the former dependence on *steering* as the basic initiation. With the parallel turn the learner is suddenly confronted with the apparently insurmountable problem of getting both skis to do something they palpably do not wish to do.

There are two possible approaches to overcoming this problem. One way would be to learn all the mechanical components of this maneuver — simultaneous edge change, heel push, and counter-rotation — and combine them with unweighting to make a turn. Given the intricacies of this description, there obviously must be a better way.

The solution was to devise a method of achieving all these aims with one single instruction or sequence of self-actuating situations. The latter is the most successful in overcoming the psychological block of getting both skis to turn through the fall line.

7 Move back into the normal traverse position in readiness for the next turn.

6 Finish the turn with a controlled degree of side-slip.

5 With the turn nearly completed, move your weight forward onto the lower ski and flex both knees to increase the edge-set.

It can be achieved by using the bump, pole plant (anticipation) and side-slip progression which, if the ground is well chosen, results in a surprisingly smooth parallel turn. Practiced first from a stationary position balanced on the crest of a small bump and then in motion on a similar bump, the sequence of knee-dip/pole plant/body twist is simple to copy. The resulting turn and skid must then be balanced by getting weight onto the front of the lower foot as the turn finishes and a new traverse slide is begun.

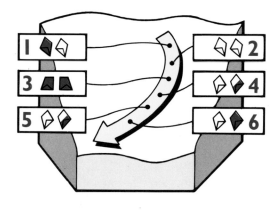

┃ *Stationary parallel turn* Stand in a stationary position on a suitable bump, with your inner pole planted just forward and beyond the apex.

2 With both skis unweighted, initiate the turn with the aid of a slight heel push.

3 As soon as you start to move, apply equal weight pressure to both skis and keep them both flat (ie not edged).

4 As both skis slide/skid smoothly off the crest and into the new direction, get ready to round up the turn by applying edge and weight pressure.

Parallel turn in motion
1 Start from the traverse position and look for a smooth place to make your turn.

2 Begin the turn by flexing your ankles and knees, swing the pole-tip forward, and anticipate with your upper body.

3 Make the pole plant and unweight the skis with a rapid extension of your legs.

4 Transfer your weight to the new outside ski during this extension phase, and begin to point your skis in the direction you want to go.

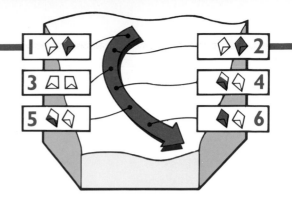

NATIONAL VARIATIONS

 Pivoting of feet already taught (see p.58). Concentrate on rhythm and interaction of body and skis.

 Step up onto inside edge of upper ski, turn hips into turn. Alternatively, open lower ski and use as braking platform, advance pole plant and step up onto upper ski.

Emphasis on down-up-down unweighting and advance pole plant on small bump.

 Three wide-stance variations taught. 1 up unweighting, pole plant, rotation and edge change (push down with upper leg, lift lower ski to join upper). 2 (for children) step up and flex onto upper ski, turn in low position without pole plant. 3 turn using advance pole plant and bump swallowing.

6 *With the turn nearly complete, get ready to repeat the process that began with figure **1**.*

5 *Now that the turn is underway, simply maintain even fore/aft balance on the outside ski.*

4 EXPERT

EXPERT

The expert skier is usually defined as one who can ski any slope and any snow condition, using a variety of parallel turns, with fluency, speed and confidence. He or she is not a racer and does not necessarily aspire to competition skiing. The border-line between an advanced intermediate and an expert is blurred and is more a case of experience rather than technical expertise.

It is a fairly common problem faced by ski schools throughout the world that the great majority of recreational skiers abandon ski school as soon as they reach a passable fluency in basic ski maneuvers. For many, ski school is too formalized and restrictive and fails to keep their interest through the lack of what they regard as adventurous skiing.

This is particularly sad at the intermediate and advanced levels because technical improvements will quickly enhance your enjoyment of skiing. If you can't perform several variations of the parallel turn, are unable to remain in balance with sudden changes in pitch, or don't understand the tactics involved in getting the most out of a ski slope, you will never experience the feeling of flight that is true expert skiing.

The freedom involves much more than flailing down the fall line, making sloppy short turns, and linked recoveries. Athletic prowess, physical strength, and guts allow many skiers to achieve that level of performance, but eventually this approach is limiting. You'll end up working more than is necessary to get down the mountain, and your improvement will reach a plateau. Don't allow this to happen to you. Familiarize yourself with the techniques discussed in this chapter, and take advantage of the advanced skiing clinics that are available at ski schools around the world. Skiing is a sport you can enjoy for a lifetime, and regardless of your ability level, you can always improve.

BUMPS AND JUMPS

A s skiing speed increases, the need to be able to control skis that show a marked tendency to get airborne becomes imperative. There are two ways of achieving this control — to swallow or absorb the bump by means of knee-flexing, so that the legs act as shock absorbers and self-leveling devices, or to promote actively a limited, controlled jump (often misleadingly called a "pre-jump").

Absorbing the jump (the French call this *avalement*) is performed by allowing your knees to ride up in time with the upward slope while, at the same time, bringing your arms, hands and poles forward but not letting the poles touch the snow.

Terrain absorption is an active movement that is actually quite simple. In essence, you should extend as you approach the bump, retract your legs at the crest, then, extend the legs again to maintain ski-snow contact on the backside. Remember two key things. First, push your feet ahead *slightly* as you approach the mogul to avoid being thrown forward as your skis decelerate while climbing up the front side of the bump. Second, keep your hands ahead so your weight doesn't end up on the tails as you accelerate down the backside.

The alternative to swallowing the bump is to make a planned and controlled jump as you cross the apex of the bump. This is done by allowing your knees to swallow the bump until the crest is reached, when your speed is great enough to propel you into the air. You keep the leg-up position at the moment of "take-off" but extend as soon as possible so that you make an early and planned contact with the snow.

It is important to remember that while you are in the air you are slowing down and the moment your skis touch the snow again you will accelerate, so you must have your weight well forward to allow for this speed increase.

The easiest way to control your skis is to keep them in contact with the snow. As soon as you get airborne you reduce your turning options and you slow down. However, there are situations in which you will need to jump to avoid obstacles, etc, so it is well worth practicing the technique.

Misjudging a jump *Failure to swallow the bump can result in an involuntary take-off. If you hit the crest of a bump stiff-legged and with your hands back 1 you run the risk of getting airborne in an unstable position 2.*

1 As you move toward the lip of the target jump, bring your arms forward in anticipation and flex both knees.

2 Continue to flex both knees so that the crest is fully absorbed and bring your arms further forward to provide extra balance.

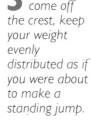

3 As you come off the crest, keep your weight evenly distributed as if you were about to make a standing jump.

4 With the lip of the jump now behind you, extend both legs to bring your skis back into contact with the snow.

5 As soon as your skis make contact with the snow, flex both knees and move your weight forward to allow for the acceleration.

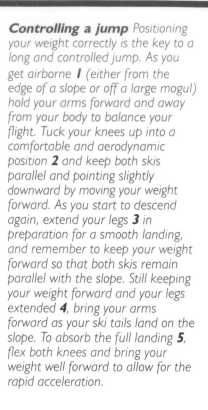

Controlling a jump *Positioning your weight correctly is the key to a long and controlled jump. As you get airborne* **1** *(either from the edge of a slope or off a large mogul) hold your arms forward and away from your body to balance your flight. Tuck your knees up into a comfortable and aerodynamic position* **2** *and keep both skis parallel and pointing slightly downward by moving your weight forward. As you start to descend again, extend your legs* **3** *in preparation for a smooth landing, and remember to keep your weight forward so that both skis remain parallel with the slope. Still keeping your weight forward and your legs extended* **4***, bring your arms forward as your ski tails land on the slope. To absorb the full landing* **5***, flex both knees and bring your weight well forward to allow for the rapid acceleration.*

BASIC CLOSED PARALLEL

The single, most difficult skill acquisition at this stage in a skier's education is the courage needed to perform a standard, basic parallel turn with both feet in close proximity. A basic wide-stance parallel requires the feet to be about hip-width apart, and in this position it is possible to initiate and steer the turn by one ski with the other following parasitically. However, a closed-stance parallel requires both legs, both feet and both skis to act simultaneously.

There is no difference in technique or in initiation of the turn; unweighting is upward, forward and rotational, and the pole plant is anticipatory. Where the difference *does* lie is that *both* skis are simultaneously changed from one edge to the new one. Weight is virtually equally distributed during the turning phase and the body is angulated — legs pushing outwards, body partly upright but leaning into the turn.

The turn is controlled by knee flexing and increased edge angle, to provide a thrust platform for the next turn or traverse.

It is a mistake to deliberately assume an angulated position; it should be the result of correct anticipation, unweighting, edge-set and balance, and becomes increasingly pronounced the higher the speed. Failure to achieve adequate angulation is frequently the result of a lack of confidence and faulty initiation. By this stage in your ski education you should be sufficiently a passenger on your skis to be able to feel free to move your body independently of your skis' movements.

It should be pointed out that holding your feet and legs together is not the goal of parallel turning. Doing this will result in earlier fatigue, in addition to making it more difficult for you to absorb terrain. What you are actually trying to do is let the legs be very close together, but still have each one ride independently throughout the turn. This is easier than you might think. All you have to do is maintain 100 percent of your weight on the outside ski, and the forces of the turn will make the inside leg swing in close to the outside.

102

5 Keeping both skis close together, increase the degree of angulation through the turning phase to encourage the necessary edge change.

7 As you come out of the turning phase settle back into the normal traverse position with shoulders pointing downhill.

6 Move into the final phase of the turn with your body lessening the degree of angulation but keeping both skis close together.

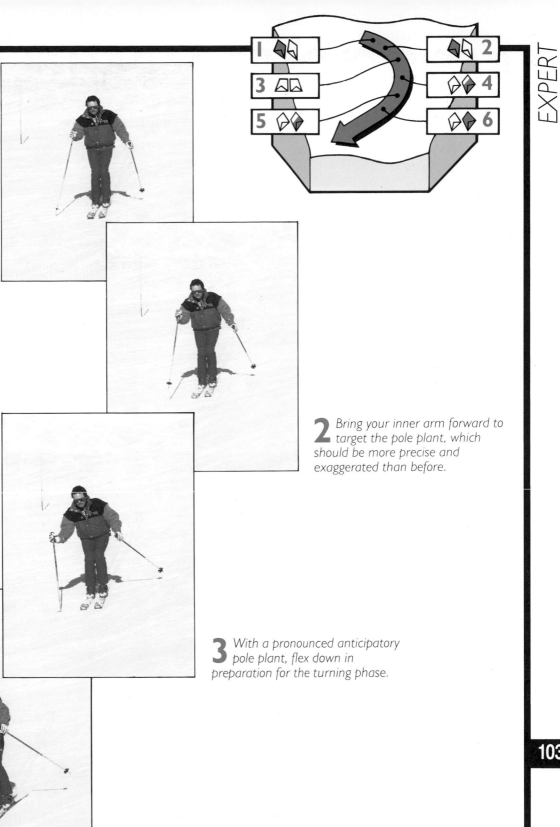

1 Approach the chosen turn location in a closed stance on a straight run.

2 Bring your inner arm forward to target the pole plant, which should be more precise and exaggerated than before.

3 With a pronounced anticipatory pole plant, flex down in preparation for the turning phase.

4 To induce the turning action, make an upward, forward and rotational unweighting and begin to lean your body into the turn.

BASIC SHORT SWINGS

A short swing is one which has a very short or non-existent traverse phase and whose average line of descent is down the fall line. The initiation and steering phase of the turn is identical with that of the basic parallel (see page 102), but instead of the turn being allowed to run its full course and degenerate into a traverse, it is halted abruptly by a strong braking action with both knees flexed and edges set more acutely into the slope. From this low position, with an accompanying pole plant in the center of the radius of the next turn, a new turn is initiated with a very positive down-thrust by both legs and a simultaneous edge change with both skis. Rhythm is essential to achieve a series of short swings, for it is the impetus of one turn which gives the drive into the following turn.

The short swing differs from the basic parallel only in the timing of the sequence of turns and the fact that the turns do not stray far from the fall line.

*The most important phase of the short swing technique is the deep and pronounced knee-flex at the end of each turn **3**, which not only acts as a braking mechanism but also forms the take-off platform for the next turn. Initiate the short swing in the same way as for a basic parallel but halt the turning phase with a deep knee-flex **5** and set both edges steeply into the slope. From this dynamic stance, initiate a new turn with a positive down-thrust **6**, pole plant **7** and simultaneous change of edge-set **8**. Seen as an overall sequence, the up-down-up unweighting should be paralleled by precise edge changes and should represent a smooth and rhythmical progression.*

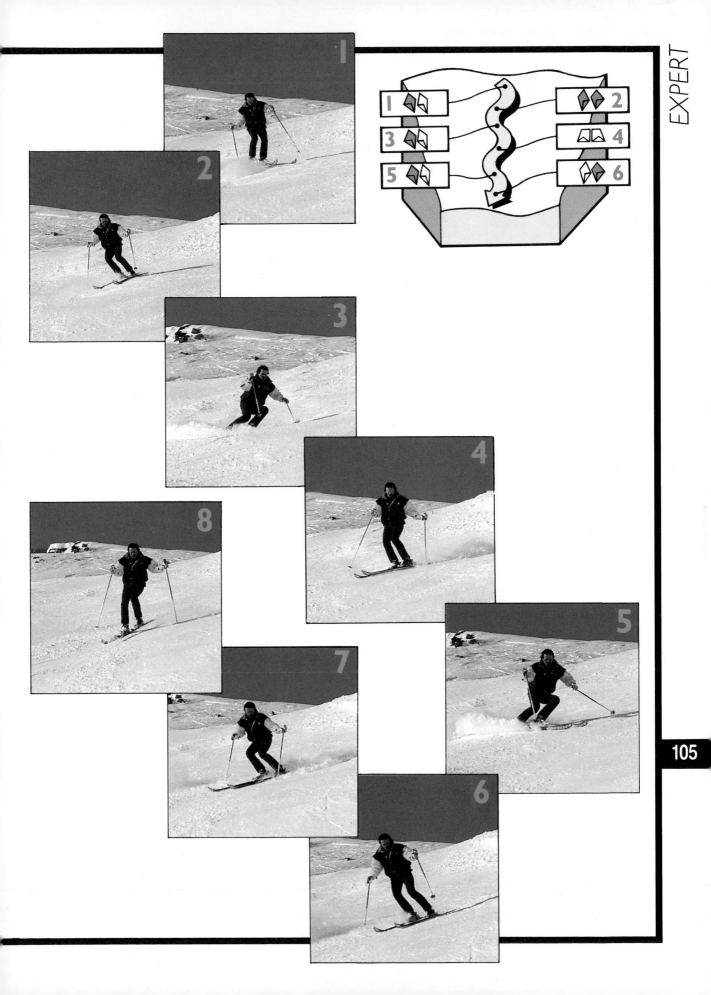

105

SUPER PARALLEL TURNS

Basically a refined version of the parallel turns discussed previously, the super parallel turn demonstrates efficiency, power, and finesse.

To perform a super parallel turn you must balance 100 percent of your weight on the inside edge of the

Super parallel turning is simply an advanced version of the parallel turn. It requires exactly balancing your weight on the inside edge of the outside ski to maximize the carving potential of your equipment.

2 *At the initiation, plant the pole lightly while transferring 100 percent of your weight to the outside ski and tipping it on edge.*

1 *To prepare for the turn, look where you're going and begin to swing your inside pole tip forward.*

3 *Continue to balance on the inside edge of the outside ski to produce a strong carving action through the finish of the turn.*

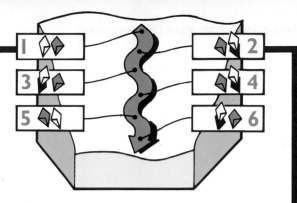

outside ski from the beginning to the end of the curve. Combined with the proper blend of edge angle, rotary power, and inward lean, you can produce turns that utilize the maximum carving power of the skis.

Super parallel skiing is only possible with exact edge engagement. The best way to learn this skill is to become aware of the soles of your feet. As you tip your ski on edge, notice that pressure increases along the inside of your foot. Throughout the turn, try to maintain that sensation of foot pressure as you increase angulation to tip the skis on edge. When you can feel the arch/heel of your foot from the beginning to the end of the curve, you are on your way to carving expert level, super parallel turns.

4 *Linking super parallel turns together depends on rhythmically changing your weight from one ski to the other.*

6 *This photo shows the exact balance on the inside edge of the outside ski that is so important to the successful execution of the super parallel turn.*

5 *Pole swing and anticipating the next turn with your eyes and upper body are also critical to the smooth linking of super parallel turns.*

107

ADVANCED SHORT SWING

Known in North America as a "rebound swing" and in France as an advanced "godille", the advanced short swing is characterized by the fact that the skis move through an arc of approximately 90 degrees from one side to the other and, to control speed down a steep slope, are never allowed to accelerate into the fall line.

To accomplish this turn you need a strong edge set (see figure 1), combined with an anticipated upper body, stabilized by a solid pole plant. The actual turn initiation is often accompanied by a very pronounced jump or hop, sometimes employing both ski poles to assist in the "take-off" on very steep ground.

Short swings can be usefully placed on the apex of any small bump, and the sequence should permit a degree of individual turn placement so as to avoid unsatisfactory ground such as rocks, ice, ruts and the like while maintaining full control of speed.

The advanced short swing is the commonest of all advanced turns and is particularly suited to steep slopes and tricky moguls.

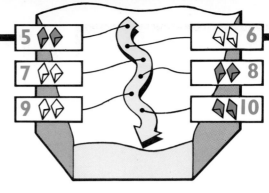

The technique for the advanced short swing differs from that for the basic short swing only in the harshness of the completion of each turn and in the exaggeration of the integral movements. On very steep slopes, the turn initiation can be assisted by a small "hop" **2** brought about by "rebounding" from the severe edge-set of the previous turn and a "blocked" pole plant **1**. To perform a successful sequence of advanced short swings it is essential that each turn is planned well in advance. You should face downhill throughout the sequence **9** and always be on the lookout for a suitable turn location **10**.

AVALEMENT

The use of variations in the terrain or snow surface to facilitate turn initiation has been mentioned before (see page 82). It is reviewed again here as it is a very important part of one of a series of other advanced parallel turns.

The actual swallowing of a bump — which is in fact nothing more than actively levelling out the terrain — is a key element in achieving a relaxed, smooth and controlled style of skiing down a wide range of slopes. Sometimes called a "compression turn," this method of turn initiation leads directly to the dramatic jet turn (see page 112).

6 *With both skis now smoothly turning, extend your legs into the falling ground and start to apply weight pressure to the lower ski.*

7 *Extend your legs further as you gain momentum off the bump and begin to resume the normal traverse position.*

I With both knees flexed, absorb the rising ground and prepare for the pole plant.

2 Continue to absorb the bump and target your pole plant just beyond and to one side of the bump's apex.

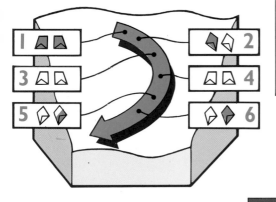

5 As you come off the crest of the bump, angle your knees into the turn and turn both skis by rotating knees and feet so that they come into line with your shoulders.

3 Make the pole plant and let your knees ride up right over the crest of the bump so that you appear to be "sitting" and leaning backward.

111

4 The apparent backward lean is the normal preliminary to the rotational turning motion that the "avalement" and pole plant have set up.

JET TURNS

The classic jet turn position, with shoulders rotating into the turn and weight shifted back onto the heels.

The jet turn is particularly effective — if very energetic — on extremely steep moguled slopes, and is also a great help in initiating parallel turns in difficult conditions, such as heavy or windblown snow.

The dynamics of the turn consist of the skis being extended or pushed (jetted) forward toward the apex of a bump at the same time as the inside pole is planted. As the directional change is entered, weight is almost entirely on the heels and the body is supported largely by the planted ski pole. As the final phase of the turn is entered, you must push yourself forward so as not to come out of the turn unbalanced.

The jet movement is also a useful way of initiating a turn when you are skiing quite slowly since it provides a means of accelerating your momentum through the turn.

5 As your skis drop away, bring your left shoulder forward and pivot your body into a central position above your skis.

6 To complete the turn, make a sharp, braking, heel skid so that you are ready to start the next turn.

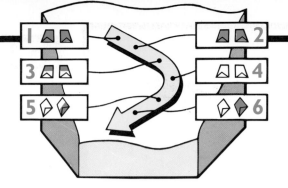

1 As you approach the target bump, absorb the rising ground and bring your inner arm forward for the pole plant. Weight should be central and completely balanced.

2 Start to shift your weight back so that you remain perpendicular to the ground while the bump is fully absorbed. Target the pole plant just beyond and to one side of the bump's apex.

3 Make the pole plant and jet your skis forward while rotating your shoulders into the turn and moving your weight onto your heels. Your body should still be perpendicular to the ground immediately beneath your feet.

113

4 With your skis now fully unweighted and your shoulders completely turned, thrust the points forward and pivot from the hips into the new direction.

CARVING A TURN

A turn is said to be carved when one ski does not skid but leaves behind a clear ski track in the snow. It is usually performed by stepping up onto the upper ski, applying weight pressure forcefully and angulating the body so as to balance exactly the centrifugal forces of the turn. It requires a positive dynamic stance and a degree of speed since it is the centrifugal push on the outside ski that enables it to carve in the required steering direction.

To get a feel for the ski's built-in turning characteristics try the following: Select a very gradual slope that's free of traffic and straight run down the fall line in an open stance. Put all your weight on one ski and tip it onto its inside edge. *Be patient* and your ski will leave the narrow, cleanly-scribed arc of a carved turn.

Even world class racers seldom make pure carved turns. Think of the preceding exercise as a goal and try to approximate the sensation. Making a strong weight commitment to the outside ski, and maintaining even fore/aft pressure on the edge, are tips that will improve your ability to carve turns.

As you apply these suggestions, remember that carving is actually a process of learning how to skid less. There are degrees of carving; exactly where a given turn fits into the continuum is a function of snow conditions, slope steepness, and the desired performance outcome.

A ski's sidecut, torsional strength and longitudinal flexibility allow it to carve through a turn. All the skier needs to do is to apply the exact amount of edge engagement and weight distribution to make it happen.

114

3 *In the middle part of the turn, angulation allows you to maintain balance and pressure on the outside ski. Combined with the strong edge angle, this causes the skis to be flexed into a round arc, referred to as "reverse camber."*

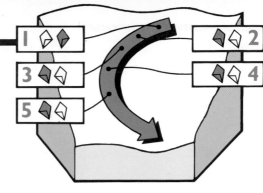

2 *Transfer your weight to the outside ski, and allow your body to cross over the skis. (Notice that the outside ski is already on edge.)*

1 *Begin the turn with a slow extension onto the outside ski and a light pole touch.*

5 *In preparation for the next turn, look where you want to go, swing the pole tip forward to prepare for another light touch, and get ready to move into the new turn.*

4 *To quit carving, gradually reduce the amount of inward lean shown in Figure 3 by allowing your body to come up over the skis.*

BANKED PARALLEL TURNS

Banked parallel turns are easy to perform, elegant and very appropriate in certain situations. Since they require little physical effort, this technique is perfect for getting down the mountain after a long day on the slopes. Banking can also be an effective way to ski certain forms of "crud snow," which is covered in Chapter 6.

Banking gets its name from the inclined position a skier assumes when making this type of parallel turn. As seen in these photographs, nearly a straight line can be drawn from the feet through the head of a skier who is banking. This relationship with the skis is very relaxed, since it allows you to stand on your skeletal structure to resist the outward forces in the turn.

Don't be misled into using this technique exclusively because there are two major drawbacks to banking. First, with your entire body leaned inside the turn, there's little chance of recovery should your skis slip. This makes banking ineffective on icy snow conditions. Second, banking from one side of the skis to the other to change edges is a relatively slow process. Consequently, banking works best with medium to longer radius turns.

3 Maintain 100 percent of your weight on the outside ski, but allow your entire body to lean into the turn. (Notice the near perfect vertical alignment of the body.)

4 As the outward forces increase more inward lean will be necessary, but don't overdo it. It is easy to get too far inside at this point and lose pressure on the outside ski.

5 Keep both knees flexed and angled into the slope to provide precisely the right edge control as you move into the final phase of the turn.

1 Prior to the initiation, flex your knees and ankles, and swing the pole tip forward to get ready for the light touch that will help start the turn.

2 By now you should have already transferred weight to the new outside ski, achieved nearly full extension in your legs, and begun the process of edge change.

6 To bring a banked parallel turn to completion, simply decrease the amount of inward lean. This is best accomplished with a smooth, gradual movement to maintain maximum glide through the finish of the turn.

7 Turn completion overlaps with turn initiation. At this point you should be mentally and physically prepared to repeat this process in the other direction.

THE WEDEL

O nce the epitome of elegant expert skiing, the wedel is rarely used today. Basically it is a "flat ski" turn performed entirely by means of a true side-to-side heel push, assisted by a rhythmic pole plant. Theoretically, the tips of the skis never leave the fall line while the tails are pivoted from one side to the other. The wedel is only really feasible on a relatively shallow slope since it provides little speed control.

The turn is performed by means of a twisting thrust by both legs through the middle of the feet, involving only a knee/leg/thigh movement pivoting at the pelvis. It is assisted by a rhythmic anticipatory pole plant and a token edge change which is just sufficient to prevent the skis from catching. There is no unweighting visible, though instinctively there may be a lightening of foot pressure for each turn.

Seen from the front on a gentle slope, you can see how the upper body is kept very still while the ski tails swing out from side to side in a smooth, rhythmic sequence. Theoretically the tips should never leave the fall line and should serve as a fulcrum around which the tails swivel.

118

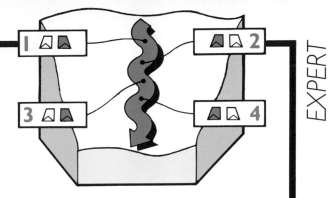

To initiate the wedel make a smooth heel and knee push **1** transmitted through the middle of your feet and pivoting at your pelvis. A light pole touch **2** helps to synchronize the side to side swinging and aids an overall rhythm, and a very minor edge change is necessary to prevent you catching an edge.

SKI RACING

The similarities between racing and recreational skiing are easy to identify. Both require snow covered slopes, equipment to facilitate sliding downhill, and the application of certain fundamentals to make the skis turn left and right. But beyond these basic tools, there is a major difference. While the recreational skier only hopes for enjoyment on the slopes, the racer wants to do exactly what the name implies. The racer's goal is to go as fast as possible from the top to the bottom of the mountain.

Racers don't really care how they "look." Their style is a result of applying the sport's fundamentals to the ski equipment that is currently available. Stylistic differences among racers within a given era are more a function of body type and relative physical strength. Ski racers are pure turning machines.

Throughout the history of skiing, racers have constantly discovered more effective, more efficient ways to turn their skis. Getting down to specifics, virtually all of the major technical breakthroughs in skiing — from stepping, to parallel, to avalement — have their roots in racing. And the impact of racing doesn't stop with skis, boots, bindings, or technique. Racing research has resulted in improved ski clothes, goggles that are less prone to fogging, and even improvement at ski resorts, thanks to the requirements of the FIS.

During the recent history of skiing, there has been increasing interest in an aspect of the sport called "recreational racing." Skiers around the world have discovered the excitement of competition. Programs such as NASTAR (the National Standard Race), ski school fun races, and organized race leagues have enlisted literally thousands of participants. And there's more to the popularity than the simple fact that it's fun to turn around gates. Recreational racing is growing because it is a great way to dramatically improve your skiing.

This chapter provides an overview of the essential information necessary to understand this aspect of the sport. It will be very useful for those interested in beginning to race on a recreational level.

The racing slalom requires an aggressive attitude and quick reactions. Notice how the racer is looking ahead toward the next turn.

In the giant slalom the racer makes longer radius turns at higher speeds. The forces generated require the skier to lean inside the turn more, while still maintaining angulation.

RACE COURSES — DOWNHILL AND SLALOM

In FIS sanctioned competitions, flexible gates must be used for SL and GS. This type of pole is much safer than the stiff bamboo poles of days past.

A race course, for all practical purposes, is a specific path down a slope, defined by a series of gates. Colored flags are attached, either to bamboo or flexible poles, and two flags of the same color constitute a single gate. To negotiate a gate successfully, the racer's ski tips and boots must pass through an imaginary line between the poles. Most forms of alpine racing alternate between red and blue gates, with the exception of downhill, where red flags are used exclusively.

Alpine ski racing has four disciplines: slalom (SL), giant slalom (GS), super giant slalom (SG), and downhill (DH). Although numerous rules govern these events in international competition, it's easiest to understand them in terms of turn shape, and average speed. Slalom racing is characterized by shorter radius turns and average speeds in the mid-30 mph range. At the other end of the spectrum, downhill requires the racers to make long radius turns and travel at speeds in excess of 60 mph down the mountain. In between are GS and SG where the speeds vary between 40 and 60 mph.

SKI RACING BASICS When two poles of a gate are set horizontally on the ski slope, it is said to be an "open gate." By contrast, a "closed" gate involves setting the poles vertically on the slope. Most alpine disciplines employ both types of gates, but closed gates are discouraged in SG or DH. Course setters avoid using closed gates in these events, since the bottom pole would pose an unnecessary danger to a racer traveling at high speed.

Of all the disciplines, slalom is the most confusing to watch for the neophyte. In addition to the open and closed gates discussed previously, slalom also incorporates gates known as "combinations." Combinations come in the forms of "hairpins" or "flushes." A hairpin is two closed gates vertically stacked above one another with a minimum of 75cm (2½ft) between the inside poles. You have the same minimum distance rule between inside poles for a flush, but this combination uses between three and five closed gates stacked vertically. Three gate flushes are most common.

According to the FIS, the gates must be taken in order, and omitting a gate results in disqualification. In

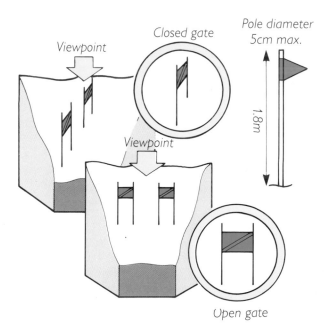

Viewpoint · *Closed gate* · *Pole diameter 5cm max.* · *1.8m* · *Viewpoint* · *Open gate*

Gates and flags *Special slalom gates consist of single poles **above right** set in pairs and identified by the alternating colors of red and blue. Giant slalom flags consist of a red or blue panel held between two poles **above left**, and the gates are also set in pairs.*

FIS regulations stipulate that the number of gates in a special slalom course is: men 55min., 75 max; women 45 min., 60 max. The number of gates in a giant slalom course is 15 percent of the vertical drop, plus or minus 5 gates.

recreational races such as ski school slaloms, single poles are often used to mark the course. In this case, each pole represents a gate, and the racer must travel around the outside of each one to successfully complete the course.

SLALOM RULES A slalom has to be skied not as a succession of single gates, but as a series of gates. The turn for each single gate is dictated by the preceding gate and the actual turn has to be so placed as to prepare you for the next gate. If you are going to be a successful slalom skier, you must commit the course to memory — especially the difficult sections.

Racers are not allowed to actually ski through the course prior to their timed run. This rule is even adhered to in club or other recreational competitions, so you must inspect the course and visualize the path the course setter has dictated. Serious racers usually inspect a slalom by sidestepping up the course, with frequent stops to memorize the turns. For the recreational racer, it is probably sufficient to sideslip alongside the gates to get an idea of what the course demands.

GIANT SLALOM This discipline differs from the "special" slalom not only in length but in the number, width and placing of the gates. The purpose of the giant slalom is to test the skier at higher speeds over varying terrain. Like the slalom it is skied "blind" (that is without a trial run) and, as in the slalom, each gate is part of the whole course and must be regarded as such, even though the actual techniques employed are technically different from those required for the more athletic and tighter slalom course. The gates, instead of being single flagged poles, consist of a broad panel held between two uprights. The coloring is similar to that used in slaloms — red and blue — and here also the skier must pass between the imaginary line drawn between a pair of flags and ski them in the prescribed order. The gates must be between 13ft and 26ft wide.

The timing of the run is usually carried out electronically, though many ski school races still use hand timing. The timing starts when the skier's feet cross the starting line or, in the case of electronic timing, when his feet break the starting-gate wand contact, and finishes when the skier's legs (or feet) cross the actual finishing line. In electronic timing, it is not possible to trigger the timing by means of ski poles, while falls are regarded as part of the run time.

*This view of the finish of the special slalom course in Schladming, Austria, ostensibly shows an impenetrable forest of poles **above**. But on closer inspection, a clear pattern and sequence of open and closed gates which utilize all the gradient and terrain variations becomes apparent.*

It is customary to have special course marshals, so-called "gate keepers," who check each skier through a set of gates and who are responsible for replacing gates which are knocked down. It is no offense to demolish a gate, providing *both* feet pass through the imaginary line joining a pair of flags in a gate.

Ingemar Stenmark — possibly the finest racer of all time — demonstrates today's slalom technique. Ingemar is literally skiing through the pole. **Right** *maintaining an aerodynamic position is extremely important in downhill. Conradin Cathomen shows perfect form at Wengen.*

Todd Brooker — shown here in the classic downhill at Wengen — has thrown caution to the wind in his effort to reach the finish line with the fastest time.

To homologate a race hill for competition, a race organizer must among other things supply a "course profile." This document gives an overview of the course's vertical drop and gradient changes

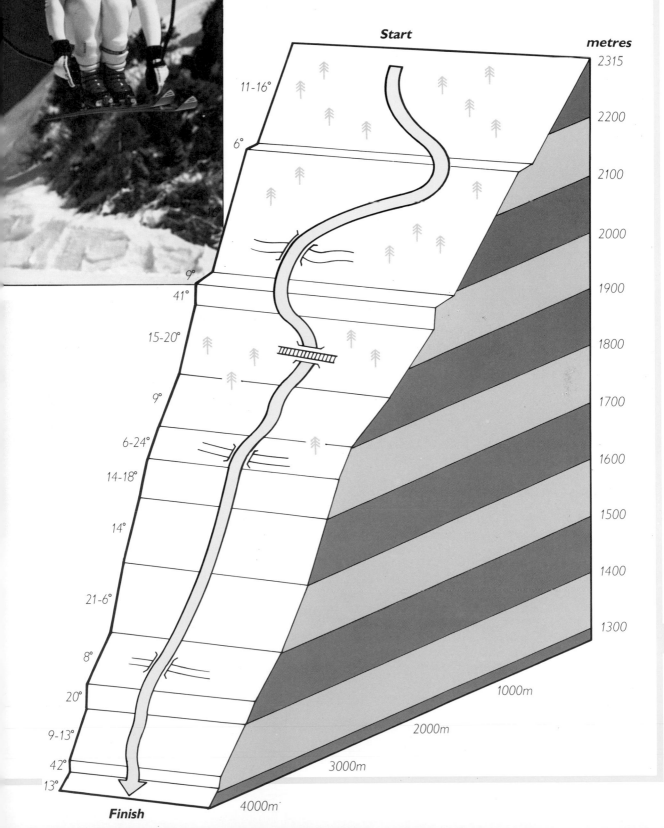

Start

metres
2315

11-16°

2200

6°
2100

16°
2000

9°
1900

41°

15-20°
1800

9°
1700

6-24°
1600

14-18°
1500

14°
1400

21-6°
1300

8°

20°

9-13°

42°

13°

Finish

1000m
2000m
3000m
4000m

THE START

Irrespective of the kind of race involved, the departure from the starting line is by means of a double pole push. The poles are placed at about the level of the ski tips, firmly embedded in the snow but loosened by means of a circular twist; this is important for otherwise there is a danger that they may catch in the snow and drag you backwards as you pass them. It is advisable to make sure that both skis are sliding freely immediately before the start signal is given. Although there is no true race start order in the case of the wand electronic timing start, the starter will normally count to a command of "go." If FIS rules are being strictly enforced, a competitor may be disqualified for starting sooner than 3 seconds before or later than 3 seconds after being told to "go."

On the command "go," you pull yourself forward on your poles, converting the pull into a push as you pass them and at the same time throwing yourself forward so that your heels tend to lift up the tails of your skis. You must be in a good forward position immediately after the start. If the run up to the first gate is lengthy, many skiers use one or two vigorous skating steps to gain speed; however care must be taken not to lose balance at this early moment of the run. The differences in time between a good and a bad start are measured in terms of fractions of seconds.

1 *Position yourself so that your shins are almost touching the wand and plant both poles firmly in the snow as close to your ski tips as possible. Flex your whole body into a crouched position in readiness.*

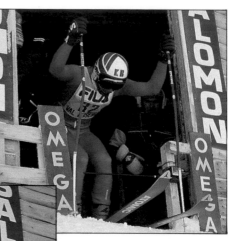

2 *On the command "go," put all your weight onto your poles and pull/ push yourself out of the starting gate so that your shins open the wand.*

3 *The force of your exit from the gate should get you momentarily airborne. Make sure that your poles clear the snow and move your weight well forward.*

THE SPEED TUCK

The purpose of the speed tuck is to achieve a good aerodynamic position. The time saved — or the extra speed achieved — is considerable, and although it is generally associated with downhill racing it is also used in giant slalom and occasionally in slalom races.

A simple way to visualize the speed tuck is to imagine your body shaped like an egg. To do this, assume an open stance and crouch down so your elbows are touching just in front of your kneecaps. Your hands should be close together, your back should be as parallel to the snow surface as possible, and the ski poles should be tucked under your arms.

When running straight downhill, distribute your weight evenly from side to side, and front to back. Getting too far forward will slow you down, and getting too far back will result in diminished control. For maximum speed, make sure you keep your skis as flat as possible on the snow. If you need to make gradual turns, rise up slightly and utilize the sidecut turns that were discussed in the preceding chapter.

The purpose of the speed tuck **left** is quite simply to increase speed. Wherever possible a racer will try and get into the tuck position. However it is very difficult to make any kind of serious turning maneuver while tucking, although long radius "sidecut" turns can be performed as this skier demonstrates.

129

SLALOM TURNS

Slalom turns are a natural development of a normal parallel step turn, though whether they are "up" or "down" depends upon the circumstances of the turn. What does become immediately apparent is the fact that at practically no point during the turn are the skis parallel and that the actual turn is performed largely on one ski, though both skis have to be brought into play as the tempo is raised.

An analysis of racing slalom turns has given rise to the "creation" of a specialist name for such turns — the "scissors christie." It is strictly speaking a misnomer in that it is not a new or different turn but merely the practical application of a time-saving step turn. Watching any slalom practice it becomes evident that a turn approached too fast results in a pushing, braking movement with the outside ski while the inner ski is still turning. The braking movement outward then becomes translated into a positive thrust by the lower ski to increase speed, and to provide a turning movement to the upper ski which is placed onto its inside edge with a very positive weight change and rotation. What has happened is that you have stepped up onto the upper ski and by edging it, weighting it and at the same time rotating in the direction of the new turn, started a tight, carved turn.

Proper pole use is a critical aspect of skiing slalom. You need to keep both hands ahead of your body at all times, and you should try to plant your inside ski pole on each turn. Pole plants should always be made with as little arm movement as possible. Think about "flicking" or "cocking" the wrist to swing the pole tip forward. Especially in steep, icy slaloms, proper pole use is a tremendous aid in maintaining control and general balance.

Beyond these basics, slalom skiing is essentially a game of quickness. Just as a mogul skier must make split-second decisions to handle a nasty bump run, the slalom racer must instantly react to the various turns and terrain changes in the course. Looking ahead to anticipate what's coming up is vital to success in this discipline.

In addition to technique, physical fitness is paramount. Linking anywhere from 45 to 74 consecutive turns down a rock-hard slope requires strong muscles and a well-conditioned cardiovascular system.

THE LINE The ideal turn is a maximum constant-radius turn; that is to say, a turn which starts high and wide, reaches its apex as close to the flag as possible and exits wide. It is exactly analogous to the line taken by a Formula I racing car, and involves the least possible centrifugal force and the least deceleration during the course

*The classic slalom turn position **above**, with the inner arm poised to brush away the pole, both skis fully edged and weighted and the outer arm held purposefully high and forward in anticipation of the next gate.*

of the turn.

Translated into slalom practice, it means that a gate is entered high and the turn largely completed before passing the inner marker of the gate. You never turn inside the gate as this would result in your exit being far too low to be able to negotiate the following gate. Your outer arm should be pointing to the apex of the next gate by the time you have passed the apex of the current gate.

Both the Swiss and Austrian ski schools devote part of the instruction time in their top class to the teaching of slalom turns but do not specifically teach racing. The American method does not include this in their advanced classes but does run special race coaching classes on demand or as a special feature of a resort's promotion.

The French schools on the other hand have a specific class, "Competition," which is devoted solely to slalom and giant slalom training. All aspects of racing are taught with particular emphasis on athletic ability. All major French resorts maintain standard slalom courses with electronic timing which are reset every day. They make a particular point of providing video sessions as they have learned that it is essentially by copying that basic racing skills are best taught and this has to be accompanied by personal, individual and visual criticism.

The key to a successful slalom (and particularly giant slalom) technique is the acceleration from one gate to another. As the gate is passed **1**, the skier has 100 percent of his weight on the outside ski, while remaining well angulated to resist the outward forces of the turn. With the gate passed **2**, you must get ready for the accelerating skating step by flexing deeply and weighting and edging your upper ski. To complete

the acceleration, step right up onto your upper ski with a skating push **3** so that this ski begins to carve, and align your shoulders with the next gate to be negotiated.

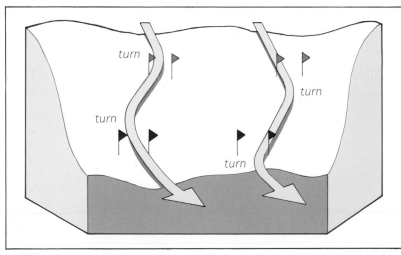

Slalom line These two theoretical lines through a pair of open gates demonstrate the difference between making good high turns before the gate and making hurried uncontrolled turns after the gate. The diagram shows that the ideal line through a gate is not necessarily the shortest distance. Turns should be made before the gate so that height is maintained thus reducing the amount of braking.

turn

turn

turn

turn

turn

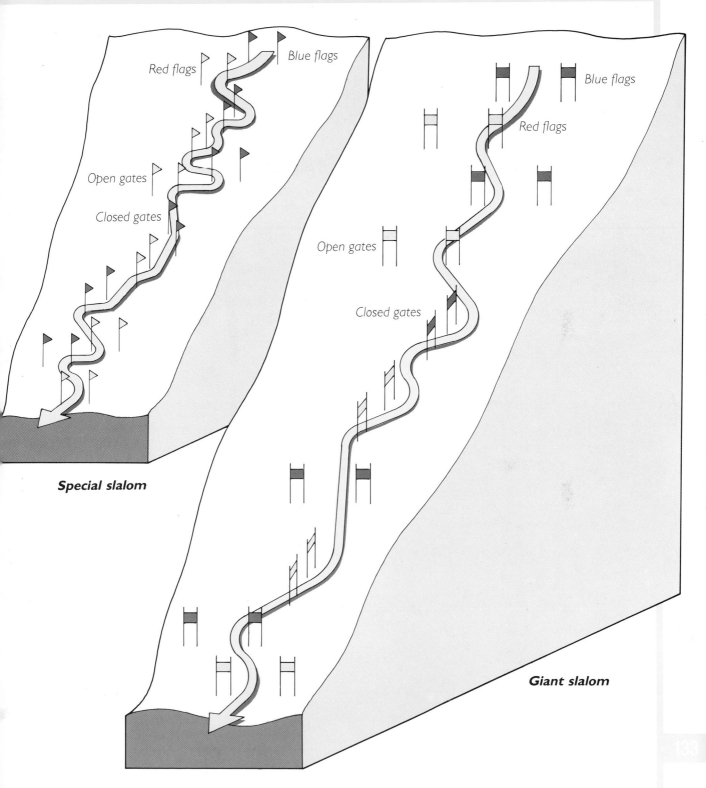

Special slalom

Red flags

Blue flags

Open gates

Closed gates

Blue flags

Red flags

Open gates

Closed gates

Giant slalom

Every year slalom techniques are refined. The current slalom stance is a highly dynamic position **left** that epitomizes the triumph of technique over style.

A typical special slalom course **above left** consists of a vertical drop of 197—241yd for men and 142—197yd for women.

A typical giant slalom course **above** consists of a vertical drop of 328–437yd for men and 328–383yd for women. The distance between gates is never less than 11yd.

SKI CRAFT

There is a great deal more to skiing than simply being able to perform with consummate skill and style the techniques of modern downhill skiing. It is not at all uncommon to find such skiers quite incompetent at mastering the most elementary choices of line or at wending their way securely through difficult snow conditions.

In the past, ski instructors made a point of taking their pupils down unfamiliar routes and little-used trails, allowing them the opportunity to apply their newly learned skills to the widest variety of conditions and situations. Today, sadly, such consideration is often ignored, the regrettable result being that far too many skiers can do no better than swing mindlessly down a slope, their turns happening at random on unsuitable snow conditions when only a short distance away lies a consecutive line of skiable snow patches which they have been unable to see or plan for.

The sum total of this knowledge can be called "ski craft". It is not always stylish nor is it necessarily fast; it does, however, contribute greatly to comfort, safety and fluency and, when legs are tired, the light is bad and the snow difficult, makes the difference between a comfortable, controlled descent and a tiring, inelegant scramble. It cannot be taught from books but, for those interested — and that should be all skiers of all categories — it is worthwhile to explore the concepts that make up ski craft. Intermediate skiers can benefit most from an understanding of ski craft for they are the most likely to be caught out by fatigue and weather and their skills may not be adequate to force the issue. For experts it can add a polish to style and form — something which becomes immediately visible as they wend their way through difficult passages and make tiring, scratchy sections appear easy and smooth.

A CHOICE OF LINE

The marked and manicured slope is no more than a very general indication of the route from A to B; it is open to innumerable variations. Some are no more than equal value alternatives; others can be more or less difficult. But within these limitations, there will be one particular line which is particularly suited to smooth, fluent skiing and which will avoid the more obvious hazards such as lumpy snow, worn patches, rocky hazards and the like. There are very few slopes that are simple, wide, even expanses; but where such slopes do occur, often after a short sharp traverse and usually leading to a narrow gully or a shoulder, there is a universal tendency to either procrastinate and turn into the slope at the last possible moment or, in a show of machismo, to bounce off the very top of the traverse, usually at a point where no proper overview of the slope is possible. Unless prior knowledge dictates otherwise, proceed along the traverse and pick your entry point where there is a smooth transition which gives you full command of the entire slope. When on the slope, observe the long turn-and-traverse lines of less competent skiers and cross these at right angles so that you can place your turn immediately after the traverse rut. Make sure to look far enough ahead so you can select a friendly path.

At some ski areas you might have ski bumps that have formed in narrow gullies. This situation may be intimidating at first because there is no apparent way to control your speed. But if the gully's banks are snow-covered it's simple. All you need to do is make turns against the side of the gully. Take advantage of the deceleration that results when you climb up the bank, try to link the turns together rhythmically, apply the basic mogul techniques discussed in Chapter 4, and gullies will be easy.

Beware of long, rutted schusses and consider how and where they end; far too often they finish in an uphill slope at the top of which a crowd will always collect, leaving you little room to stop and possibly committing you to a blind approach to whatever follows.

An analysis of your route should recall a smooth progress with no unplanned, emergency turns; no skiing yourself into an uncomfortable corner; and no compulsive, continuous use of a single turn. Every little part of a slope has its own ideal kind of turn, and any given stage should be dealt with on merit, and the relevant technique applied.

*Gullies can be a lot of fun to ski down, particularly if they are steep and wide **above**. However, before starting down a gully be sure as to which direction you will need to exit in and where any likely narrow sections are.*

Any stretch of slope has its own natural line, whether it is demarcated by trees, moguls or gullies.

Trees should be approached with care. Wherever possible make your turns above a tree, well clear of the snow hole or "tree well" that invariably lies downhill of the base of the trunk.

Moguls are always an exciting route but you can increase the pleasure if you look ahead and plan your turns. Try and vary your turns but if you are feeling really adventurous make them on top of the moguls.

If you want to show off your short swing technique look out for any gullies, but try not to ruin other people's fun by hogging the center.

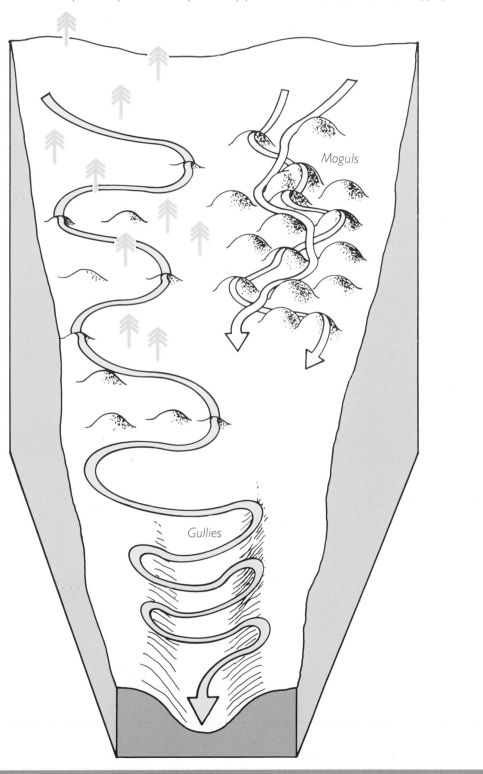

Moguls

Gullies

MOGULS, TRAVERSES AND PATHS

This unholy trio can be found on any slope in any country. The first two are the result of the passage of many skiers down a single, unavoidable route. The third is a result of the natural contours and geography of mountains, valleys and tree lines.

MOGULS Strangely, only North American ski schools have paid consistent and detailed attention to the problem of mogul fields; other schools have contented themselves with indicating techniques for skiing them.

Mogul fields are not unavoidable, and you should examine the slope before starting down it. Inevitably, the outside edges will be less moguled than the center and, what is more, these outside edges will have softer snow conditions.

There are basically three ways to ski through moguls. Least preferable is the "traverse and turn" approach. Often selected by less skilled skiers, this method is guaranteed to result in frustration and exhaustion. The next option is to ski through the troughs. In large, round bumps this can work well, but in smaller, sharper moguls there may not be room to stay in this line. Finally, you can ski the "tops" of the bumps. This line requires aggressive, explosive moves to fly from one mogul top to the next. In practice, most experts ski a combination of a line through the troughs and one that passes over the tops.

TRAVERSES Traverses, particularly if they are rutted, can cause problems. Consider it this way — the purpose of the exercise is to get down the mountain; as most skiers have timorously side-slipped and tended to move up the slope, the best and softest snow is just below the lowest traverse track. Move there determinedly, and when you reach the steep little gully around which you have to ski, turn into the gully (as if it were uphill) and cross it as if you were on a contour line.

PATHS For many skiers narrow paths, usually through woods with steep sides and poor snow, pose serious problems. Assuming you are not of the demonstrative, showy variety who wedels down the center more or less out of control, your solution is very simple — use only the outside edge, no matter how steep, wooded or apparently unfriendly it may seem. On this edge you will find all the snow missing from the center, you can stem with the outside foot, right off the path, in complete control thus missing the fallers and all those who have caught a ski tip on the steep upper slopes. And

Steep mogul fields are either your personal nightmare or your idea of fun. The key to really enjoying a steep descent is to plan ahead. Before starting your run choose a suitable vantage point and study the mogul pattern. Depending on how adventurous you are feeling, you can either ski down the margins, make looping turns following the contour line or throw caution to the wind and short swing down the center **above.**

All resorts like to boast horrifyingly steep mogul fields, but the less experienced skier need not be disheartened. Although this field **right** *may look impossibly steep from this angle, careful turn planning can reduce it to a perfectly manageable run.*

when you come to the equally inevitable hairpin, turn through the tightest, inside angle unless the path is clear of skiers and you can risk a controlled slide around to the new outside edge. When you are skiing freely down a soft, comfortably straight path, keep your mind firmly fixed on your skiing; if you do not you will inevitably catch an edge. If you must pass another skier, do so on the outside and remember — the slower skier has the right of way.

There are many famous steep gullies and slopes which start with a knee-trembling leap off a rocky outcrop or cliff **above**. However, this is not something for the inexperienced and even experienced skiers should not attempt such a leap unseen.

STEEP SLOPES, ICE, SLUSH AND CRUST

Steep slopes are either the ultimate thrill, or the final nightmare. For recreational skiers who like a challenge and for ordinary skiers who, through one cause or another find themselves confronted with what appears to be an unskiable precipice, there are certain basic techniques which will overcome the difficulties with ease and style.

When the slope is extremely steep you must make a quick, deliberate turn initiation. Casually guiding your skis into the fall line will result in quick acceleration and will probably cause you to lose control. The basic technique is: turn smoothly and rapidly through the fall line.

As you complete the turn, make sure your hands stay forward. This really helps you keep up with the skis and makes it easier to swing the pole tip forward in preparation for the next turn. Doing this properly is extremely important for success on the steep. The pole plant helps maintain your weight on the downhill ski, in addition to being a vital component of the edge set, which allows speed control.

The basic technique is to step the turn with the outside (uphill) ski, placing it at an acute angle to the traverse, pointing as far as possible towards the new direction. At this point weight is entirely on the lower ski and as soon as the outside ski has been positioned, lean forward and downhill as if you intended to dive off the slope; you will turn smoothly through the fall-line.

ICE Regrettably perfect snow conditions can rarely be guaranteed, so it is advisable to be prepared for the variety of difficult snow surfaces that are commonly encountered and which place added demands on your technique.

Strictly speaking, ice is extremely hard snow, caused either by wind, thaw and freeze or by the continual passage of skiers. True ice (i.e. clear, frozen water) is extremely difficult to ski, even with razor-sharp edges and flawless technique. The greatest problems with ice (apart from being extremely uncomfortable to fall on) are the lack of control at the exit from a turn and the inability to hold a traverse. Both situations are caused by a combination of the following: the skis are too soft, both longitudinally and torsionally, so that a true edge cannot be maintained; the edges are blunt and do not cut into the surface sufficiently to give a true purchase (but this is less common than supposed and is mostly the justification given for what is in fact the third reason); lack of skill and technique.

The margin between a controlled ski and one which has lost adhesion to the surface is extremely slim and can be crossed simply by over-edging, brought about either through anxiety or a mistaken belief that more edging means greater purchase. The practical answer is to ski exceedingly delicately, using the absolute minimum of edge and to avoid trying to hang onto a traverse too long. By constantly turning before the ski slides away (and planning your route several turns ahead) it is possible to ski down an icy slope in control.

SLUSH Slush either comes in the form of over-melted spring snow, or sticky, porridge-like new snow, sometimes called "mashed potatoes." Neither condition is as easy to ski as perfect packed powder, but this snow is certainly manageable. All you need are the correct techniques.

Consider the two main difficulties posed by slushy snow. Slush produces significant turning resistance to the skis which makes it difficult to get them pointed in any new direction. "Slush piles" often develop in this snow condition, which may disturb your balance when you run into them.

To accommodate the difficulties of slush, try the following. First, get aggressive, particularly at the turn initiation. You must accentuate your movements to get the direction change started. Try to unweight your skis and steer with both legs. Once you get the turn going, avoid getting too far forward. By staying off the fronts of your skis, you will be able to ride up and over the slush piles.

CRUST As the name implies, "crust" is a condition that involves a layer of frozen, tightly packed snow crystals on its upper surface. If the crust layer is deep and/or very strong, it poses no particular problems since it will support your weight. Don't worry about skiing on a solid crust. It's like skiing any hardpack.

But if you encounter "breakable crust," *watch out!* This snow condition is treacherous and it provides a major challenge to even the most expert skiers.

Consequently, try to avoid skiing slopes that have a breakable crust. It is extremely frustrating to do linked crashes down any run, and this snow condition is downright dangerous. Regardless of your ability, the sanest approach to a crust-covered slope is the traverse/turn method. Select a shallow traverse so your speed remains slow, and make a turn into the hill when you reach the other side of the slope. The key to making this turn at the end of the traverse is to maintain even fore/aft weight distribution on the skis, and to bank slightly into the hill. After the first traverse, turn around in the other direction, and repeat the process until the conditions change, or you have reached the bottom of the run.

*Skiing steep powder slopes **left** is actually easier than it looks. Powder snow helps to hold your skis and the steepness helps in the initiation of turns, but remember that the steeper the slope, the greater the down-up-down unweighting sequence must be and the more positive the anticipatory pole plant.*

The easiest type of turn to use is the basic step turn with the uphill ski (see page 88). Other suitable turns are the jump turn or a modified form of short swing.

141

POWDER SNOW SKIING

*Deep powder **left**, **right** is arguably the most exciting, dramatic and satisfying there is — and it is not nearly as difficult as some intermediates think. While there is no such thing as deep powder technique, it is also true that a powder snow turn will accentuate any errors in basic turning skills.*

For many skiers powder snow is the ultimate pleasure. It is also considered, possibly falsely, as a highly specialized technique which (in all ski schools) is reserved for the top, expert classes (though, interestingly, the Swiss School advises intructors to take low intermediates onto easy powder snow slopes as the skiing there, quite correctly, is easier).

For many intermediates powder snow is a psychological negative, largely, if not entirely, due to the fact that skis are invisible and the skier has to depend upon "foot-feel" and acquired, instinctive skills. A further factor is the quite unnecessary image powder snow skiing has acquired as being something mystical to which only the chosen few are fit and capable of mastering and enjoying. A professional tennis coach who was also a former championship slalom skier once compared getting people onto powder to getting a tennis novice to come up to the net. Unless this was introduced very early in schooling, an unbridgeable gap remained between base-line and net. Much the same can be said about getting the inexperienced intermediate to even contemplate venturing onto powder snow.

This reluctance is unfortunate because powder skiing is one of the true joys of the sport. Deep snow provides a weightless, floating sensation that comes about as close as a human can get to the feeling of flying without growing wings. Like other aspects of "ski craft," all that's needed are the proper techniques.

The basic requirement for successful powder skiing is a well executed parallel turn. Although various forms of stepping or plowing are certainly possible in powder snow, parallel turns are definitely the easiest. If you are having difficulties with parallel turns, please review Chapter 4.

When making parallel turns in powder conditions, keep in mind the following suggestions. Number one is rhythm. Establish a steady cadence and you'll find it much easier to link one turn to the next. Second, *always* begin a powder run by heading straight down the hill for a short distance, then turn to the left or right. This "half turn" approach is much easier than starting out in a traverse, which requires a complete turn with almost no momentum. Third, to maintain balance and control in powder, you must have even fore/aft weight distribution on the skis. Don't sit back. Finally, use a pronounced down-up motion to help unweight the skis during each turn initiation. This motion is especially important in very deep or heavy snow where the resistance to turning can be extreme.

*In very deep snow **above** you must become adjusted to a kind of "floating" sensation as your ski tips pierce the surface.*

NATIONAL VARIATIONS

Bring skis up by retracting legs. Turn legs in retracted position and extend down during the turn.

Emphasis on down unweighting, no back weighting and evenly balanced skis.

Lean back at slow speeds. Let your tips float to the surface at high speeds.

Emphasis on back weighting only when ski tips break surface.

Skiing powder snow *In very general terms powder snow skiing requires rhythmically linked, short radius turns, **2** combined with a very balanced stance in which the skier attempts to stand in the middle of his foot. The deeper the snow the harder it is to initiate turns and the greater the danger of your ski tips diving down under the surface. Pole plants **6** need to be more pronounced and you must promote an active and possibly exaggerated up-down-up knee flexing.*

SNOW CRAFT AND AVALANCHES

All snow, after it lands on the ground, starts life as what is often mistakenly called powder snow. It would be more accurate to talk about "new snow," keeping the term "powder snow" for a very distinct form of new snow. Snowflakes can be wet or dry, depending on the temperature. Below about 23°F the snow will consist of small dry flakes and will not make a useful snowball. Above this temperature it will become increasingly wet, the size of the snowflakes will increase and each flake will carry a certain amount of free water.

The moment the flake touches the ground it begins to change. There are two types of change — destructive and constructive metamorphosis. The former is the more obvious. To begin with, the flake loses its distinctive sharp spikes, becoming increasingly rounded and linked into neighboring flakes. At the same time it shrinks in volume and this shrinkage compresses the snow so that it becomes crusted. Within this crust, whether near the surface or deep under fresh layers of snow, the ice crystals begin the constructive phase of metamorphosis when the snow begins to give off increasing amounts of water vapor which, in turn, re-crystalize into large, often cup-shaped, crystals, while the mass of the snow becomes a formless aggregate of ice shapes. With a further rise of outside temperature (the temperature inside a snow layer is pretty uniformly 28 to 30°F) the ice shapes melt, congeal and eventually finish up as wet, coarse slush.

The greatest effect on the surface is that caused by wind combined with temperature changes, of which wind is the more important. Snow which is moved by air (freighted) undergoes a very curious change — once it lands on the ground again, it solidifies instantly, a fact that can be seen whenever a snow-blower is in action. Even very slight air movement is sufficient to change new snow dramatically — it becomes tough and unskiable.

The following snow surfaces and variations are those most commonly encountered by skiers:

Windcrust is the surface produced by the passage of air over new snow; it may be only paper thin but can become considerably thicker and increasingly impossible to ski over. It is frequently marked in ripples and waves and can be seen in patches in the middle of large areas such as glaciers.

Snow slab is snow which has been freighted by the wind and is found in the lee of any mound, ridge or bump. It is the cause of the most dangerous form of avalanche — slab avalanche. Snow slab is caused by the

*Glaciers **above** are formed where winter snowfall exceeds summer melting. As the snow layer thickens, solid ice is formed by the recrystalization of the accumulated snow. This ice-fall in Chamonix, France, is an exciting descent but requires very careful and exact turning.*

shrinkage and melting of the loose snow cover in such a manner that the surface is under tension and there is an air pocket under the actual slab. When the surface is breached the entire cover disintegrates and slides. Wind slab eventually disintegrates and the surface then acquires an orange-peel look and is eminently skiable.

Marble crust is dull-colored and is found in irregular patches on the windward side of slopes where the wind has polished and scrubbed the surface. The areas are frequently dome-shaped and surrounded by softer skiable snow. Marble crust offers no purchase to skis despite its often roughish surface.

Ice crust is the result of the freezing of surfaces after a thaw. It is commonly known as plain "breakable crust" and is difficult and treacherous to ski.

Sun crust is found in the spring on sun-exposed slopes of some steepness and is easily recognized by the glint and reflection of the paper thin ice layer over the snow. Below this very friable crust, the snow always offers extremely good skiing, but the noise of the breaking crust (like glass) and its destructive sharpness makes it, psychologically, difficult to ski.

Powder snow in its classical form is extremely rare in the Alps and rarely of long duration. However, in areas of extreme dryness and low temperatures, such as the North American Rockies, the powder snow is extremely light, does not consolidate easily and is perfect for skiing. In the northern hemisphere, north- and east-facing slopes are the most advantageous but at the same time hold a continual danger of avalanche.

Spring snow is possibly even more pleasant and certainly easier to ski. It is formed by the repeated freezing and melting of the upper layer of the snow surface. It forms gradually, first on the south and west slopes and lastly on the northern and eastern exposures, providing there is sun and no wind; temperature is unimportant, though ideally it should be just below freezing. By mid-afternoon it will have degenerated into spring slush which will freeze instantly when the sun leaves it or a wind springs up. The nearer to a right angle the slope exposure is in relation to the sun, the quicker spring snow will form.

Spring snow conditions bring with them one embarrassment. It is not uncommon to find, at the end of a slope in perfect condition, where the slope flattens, a problem nicknamed "Pooh-traps." Here unwary skiers will find that their skis disappear under them, buried in a mass of spring snow, the lower layers having been melted away leaving a great air-hole.

AVALANCHES

Avalanches are the result of snow which has become unstable on a slope steep enough (and that is a very slight slope indeed) to permit the snow to slide. They can be spontaneous in the case of a rapid and prolonged thaw or continuous, very heavy snowfall. As far as is known they are not set off by shouts but can, very occasionally, be triggered by the passage of an animal.

As a very rough classification, three types of avalanche can occur:

Dry, powder snow avalanches are the result of excessive snowfall in very cold, windless conditions. Their destructive power lies in the supersonic air displacement they cause which, hurricane-like, flattens everything in its unpredictable course. Humans and animals die by suffocation and drowning due to the penetration of the very fine snow particles into the lungs.

Wet snow slides are the result of saturation by meltwater and are characterized by their narrow, point-like origin and their totally predictable path. They usually consist of the entire snow cover and are mixed with trees, wood, grass and mud. When they come to rest, the snow congeals into a concrete-like mass which can take all summer to disappear. They are slow-moving, make a loud hissing sound and can often be avoided, for they flow, river-like, down predestined gullies.

Slab avalanches are the commonest and concern skiers the most. They originate on lee slopes of any size, no matter how small, and can be recognized by the irregular, fragmented snow blocks which litter their end.

Searching the path of an avalanche for victims is a long and tiring task **above**. *The long sounding rods are prodded into the snow searching for the feel of a body, and the process has to be done with meticulous precision and discipline.*

These blocks do not consist of the whole snow cover but only the freighted, altered snow resulting from a previous snowfall accompanied or followed by wind. The surface can often be recognized by its smooth, dead color. When tapped it can sound hollow and when the surface is breached, there is a dull thud or even a quite loud bang as a crack appears, running across the slope at very high rates of speed. There is a moment's delay before the snow starts to slide, breaking up into blocks which, in turn, override each other and, in the case of a long slope and soft blocks, will eventually rise into the air in the form of a rapidly moving snow-particle cloud, often giving rise to a mistaken identification of a powder avalanche. The human danger lies in the weight and speed of the blocks which quickly overwhelm skiers and frequently cause severe or mortal injuries.

There is only one certain safe behavior in cases of avalanche danger — go home, do not ski off-course when the danger is posted at the bottom of ski lifts, do not ski slopes closed for this reason and listen to the advice of the professionals. Should you be caught by an avalanche the best course of action is to traverse to the closest edge of the slide as fast as possible. If the snow overwhelms you, do not panic, keep your mouth closed, attempt swimming motions and try to keep a space clear about your chest as the snow compacts and compresses. For those witnessing an avalanche accident, remember that speed is of the utmost importance; mark the place where the victim(s) was last seen scan the scene for any clothes and skis and go for help.

Do not trample all over the avalanche as this confuses the scent for the dogs. Listen for any shouts for help and if you are going to search for the victim, start downhill from where they were last seen.

SKI MOUNTAINEERING AND TOURING

Ski mountaineering and Alpine ski touring is the oldest form of Alpine ski activity for the simple reason that in the years between the late nineteenth century and early 1930s this was the only way you could acquire sufficient altitude from which to ski downhill. However, by 1960 it was almost an eccentricity, largely on account of the equipment which had increasingly become inimical to the requirements of the tourer and mountaineer. The equipment of the day was such that you could not walk in the boots, the bindings allowed no free heel movement, the skis made the attachment of climbing skins almost impossible and, where once every ski instructor was also a high mountain guide, the new generation of teachers and ski schools confined their attention to the regular slopes.

Recently there has been a very strong movement back to the calm, quiet pleasure of lonely peaks and passes, the equipment manufacturers have found sufficient outlets to permit them to redesign for this specialist requirement and many ski clubs are now actively sponsoring the discipline.

The skiing requirements of the ski tourer and mountaineer are quite demanding. Safety and control are the dominant features and it is essential that you are fully competent in all the basic maneuvers — snowplow/stem turns, stem-christies (basic turns) and basic parallels, all of which must be skill-perfect in all snow conditions. In addition, the art of kick-turning on steep slopes (both uphill and downhill) is essential. Physical fitness and stamina are required so that a climb of three to four hours is not exhausting, and practice in skiing with a heavy rucksack is an advantage.

EQUIPMENT Essential equipment consists of boots stiff enough to take safety bindings but also soft enough to permit comfortable uphill walking, while still giving the necessary support for downhill skiing. Most ski tourers use specialist light, shortish, soft skis suitable for all snow conditions. Specialist bindings are required which will permit a full heel-lift for climbing but which can be set to lock the heel for skiing. "Skins" made of nylon or mohair are strapped or stuck to the ski base and removed for the downhill sections. Clothing is generally knee-length climbing trousers, heavy knee socks, leg gaiters, overpants and a good quality jacket. A modern rucksack, sitting high on the back and provided with straps and loops for carrying skis, is essential. For overnight stops and week-long, hut-to-hut trips, a sleeping bag is handy, as are basic provisions.

Ski mountaineering expeditions (ie tours which take skiers to the highest possible point after which normal climbing on foot completes a route usually including lengthy glacier passages) require, in addition to normal ski equipment, the addition of *Harscheisen* (snowblades attached to the side-walls of the skis for traversing icy slopes). Standard Alpine equipment — crampons, ice axe, rope, pitons, and the like — is normally carried on all ski mountaineering trips. Where long glacier sections are planned, the use of a comfortable rope harness is advisable.

TOURING VERSUS MOUNTAINEERING Ski touring, essentially a high-winter undertaking, is concerned with the lower mountains and passes which can generally be reached after two or four hours' climb from a resort or mountain village. The downhill part is frequently on a route different from the ascent and commonly to a different end point.

Ski mountaineering, on the other hand, is concerned more with the genuine mountain peaks. Many of the great ski mountaineering routes are week-long, hut-to-hut expeditions. The time for ski mountaineering is early summer, when the days are long and the temperatures at high altitude are bearable. It is also at this time of the year that the glacier crevasses have been snow-bridged by the spring snowfalls and high winds that usually accompany them.

Bindings *To facilitate climbing, touring bindings are designed to allow the boot heel to lift freely. But they can also be fixed to the ski so that they function in the same way as downhill bindings.*

Rucksack *A ski mountaineering rucksack sits very high on your back and has side straps for carrying skis.*

Skis and skins *Skis are light and short. Climbing skins are attached with a special wax.*

Boots *These must be soft enough to permit uphill walking and yet stiff enough to provide support for downhill skiing. They usually have a profiled, non-slip sole.*

Rope and harness *For long glacier sections, a climbing rope and harness is essential.*

149

THE HAUTE ROUTE

The gentle climb up the Glacier d'Otemma **above** is a good start to a very long day and leads eventually to the Cabane des Vignettes.

Moving from left to right, the red line marks ascending sections and the orange line marks descending sections.

The route can be skied either from Argentière in France or from Saas Fee in Switzerland, although the west to east permutation is generally considered preferable. The Aiguille du Tour is a popular and easy peak on this stage of the route.

The stage from Champex to Bourg St Pierre is negotiated by taxi or bus. It is usual to spend a night for rest and reprovisioning in either of these two villages before starting the long two-day section to the Vignettes hut or Arolla village.

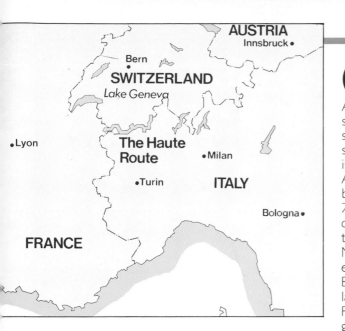

O f all the great ski mountaineering routes, the Haute Route linking Chamonix in France and Saas Fee in Switzerland, across the highest of the Alps, has most caught the imagination of adventurous skiers. It was first conceived in 1907 by a great Swiss skier and mountaineer, Marcel Kurz. The classic route starts in Saas Fee and finishes in Argentière in France. It is 75 miles long and takes between 10 and 14 days. Accommodation is in untenanted huts, so food has to be carried for several days until it can be replenished in Zermatt, Arolla and Champex or Bourg St Pierre. It is customary to include a number of major peaks during the course of the full route — Adler and Strahlhorn, Monte Rosa, Pigne d'Arolla and Aiguilles Doré, for example. The traverse can conveniently be broken at Bourg St Pierre on the St Bernard Pass. Recently, owing largely to the commercialization of the traverse by French Guides, it has become customary to start in Argentière and finish in Zermatt, without including any summits.

The route is by no means fixed and there are innumerable variations and abbreviations. It should not be attempted before May and every care should be taken not to be trapped by adverse weather in the Chanrion or Vignette huts, for neither has a safe, all-weather escape route.

The Haute Route is fairly strenuous and includes several steep ascents and descents. Famous among these is the Col du Mont Brulé which, if moving toward Zermatt from the Vignette can, on a hot morning, break the heart of many skiers. An average day's climb on this route will never be less than four hours and where possible the timing is so organized as to occupy the early hours of the morning. Skiing usually finishes by midday when the snow is becoming soft and unsafe. Starts are frequently at day-break or earlier. The route can only safely be abandoned at Bourg St Pierre or Champex and at Arolla and Zermatt.

*Grand Combin **above**, one of the highest peaks, is occasionally climbed by some of the more adventurous ski mountaineers.*

Arolla

Cabane
des Dix
2928

Glacier de Pièce

Pigne d'Arolla

Cabane des
Vignettes
3158

3637 Mont Collon

Petit Mont
Collon

3716 L'Eveque

Glacier d'Otemma

Mont Brûlé 3585

3724 Tête Blanche

Stockje Glacier

Schönbiel Hütte
2694

Matterhorn

Tête de
Valpelline 3802

Matterhorn

Ski-lift

Breuil

From the Cabane de Chanrion it is a very long 14-hour trek to Zermatt over the Col Mont Brulé. Skiers coming from Zermatt or Saas Fee usually include the Pigne d'Arolla on their way from the Vignettes hut to the Chanrion.

A delightful little excursion at this stage is to visit the Cabane des Dix near Arolla.

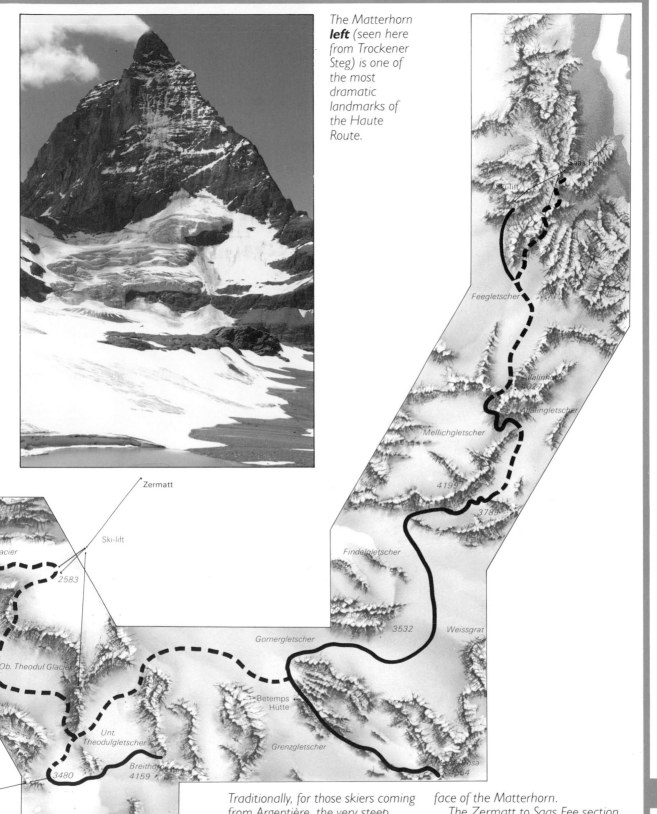

The Matterhorn **left** (seen here from Trockener Steg) is one of the most dramatic landmarks of the Haute Route.

Zermatt

Ski-lift

Glacier

2583

Ob. Theodul Glacier

Unt. Theodulgletscher

Breithorn 4159

3480

Gornergletscher

Betemps Hütte

Grenzgletscher

Feegletscher

Saas Fee

Ski-lift

Allalinhorn 4027

Allalingletscher

Mellichgletscher

4199

3789

Findelgletscher

3532

Weissgrat

Monte Rosa 4564

Traditionally, for those skiers coming from Argentière, the very steep climb to the Col Mont Brulé is the worst section of the route, but it is more than compensated for by the view of the unfamiliar, hidden west-face of the Matterhorn.

The Zermatt to Saas Fee section is rarely attempted by skiers from Argentière. But for those starting from Saas Fee it is quite the most dramatic.

153

7 CROSS-COUNTRY SKIING

It is one of the paradoxes of skiing that the oldest, in fact the original, ski discipline should have been the last to become popular. It is very understandable. The obvious excitement and pleasure of speed, freedom and skill was an inescapable attraction for those seeking recreation and enjoyment in a winter sports resort, and the comparison with the apparently effortful slog across flat country on skis was too pedestrian an occupation to attract much interest. In any case it was far too close to the arduous progress on foot which snowy winters made only too common a task in everyday life to be considered an occupation for vacation-time.

It should not be forgotten that it was Alpine, downhill skiing which was the "skiing" developed and written and talked about in Alpine Europe while "real" skiing (at least in the Scandinavian view) was an occupation limited to Scandinavia, and even there was by no means a universal winter occupation. In the 1920s, despite the fame of Norwegian ski jumpers in the wider world, skiing was, for the Norwegians at least, a peasant occupation which a very few, notably in Oslo, had made a fashionable eccentricity. In the Telemark and Bergen areas skiing was an essential form of winter transport, not a recreational activity. Most of Sweden knew little of skiing and in Finland it had a definitely military connotation.

These perceptions began to change when cross-country (XC) skiing became popular in the 1970s. Particularly in the United States, Nordic skiing grew dramatically. It seemed that wherever snow fell in that country — from the east coast to the west coast, and many places in between — Americans were discovering the joy of "skinny skiing."

The excitement about Nordic skiing in the US can be attributed to several factors. Number one, cross-country skiing is an excellent form of aerobic exercise. With so many citizens concerned about their health, cross-country skiing was recognized as an ideal way to improve physical fitness while enjoying the beauty of the great outdoors. Secondly, most people learn the basics of Nordic skiing very quickly. Lighter weight equipment and the simplified techniques of this form of ski sport provide an easy entry point and a high success rate. Finally, cross-country skiing grew in the US because it is generally less expensive. The rates for trail passes at a cross-country skiing center are roughly one-third those charged for downhill skiing, and a complete equipment package can be purchased for half the price of Alpine gear.

The European development was, inevitably, different and slower. Here

the emphasis was, notably from Germany, on health. *Langlaufer Leben Länger* (cross-country skiers live longer) was the cry and the commercial interests were very quick to develop an entirely new and apparently limitless market for the equipment, clothing and venues of the "new" sport. It came at a very timely moment when the turnover of ski sports equipment had reached a temporary lull. The equipment makers were quick to offer their new range of skis and poles, the clothing makers discovered a wonderful new outlet for a completely fresh range of sports fashion and pre- and après-ski wear.

The Swiss were less extreme. During the war years they had coined the phrase *Das ganze Volk fährt Ski* (the whole country skis) in order to encourage people to get outside and thus save domestic fuel. Cross-country skiing was an obvious target as it required the least in terms of infrastructure. The lowlands of Switzerland are an ideal area for this kind of skiing and it had been a semi-dormant sport in many such areas — notably the Jura and the hills of Einsiedeln near Zurich. The French ignored the entire development for many years and still regard the *ski de fond* as a kind of aberration even though they have some magnificent venues in the Puy du Dôme, the Vosges and the French Jura.

This, now major, ski discipline has coined a new vocabulary and with this vocabulary has come the acceptance of Nordic skiing as an important and by no means deviant aspect of ordinary recreational skiing. It is practiced on the *loipe*, graded blue, red and black according to difficulty (how much up and how steep down) and signposted with the relevant lengths — 3mi, 6mi, 9mi, and more. There are special waxing huts and resting places, rules and regulations concerning discipline, one-way traffic, properly organized Nordic ski schools and an extensive equipment-rental system. It is a fully commercial operation, and there is probably not a single ski resort in the Alps which has not got a *loipe* of some length — even if it is only a short little oval around the local playing fields.

But the great spread of interest and participation has brought with it many problems not obviously visible to the layman. The preparation and maintenance of the *loipes* is expensive both in men and machinery and many resorts are still studying means by which a charge can be made for the use of the tracks. Furthermore they are having problems with walkers spoiling the carefully machined tracks, and even more serious, the fouling of the trails by dogs. Perhaps more worrying, however, is the recreational spread of a new technique, the Siitonen step or racing skate step where, as opposed to the customary diagonal gait, one ski is skated with every step. The result not only destroys the *loipe* track but makes passing almost impossible unless the customary double tracks are far wider apart. The suggestion has been made by the German Ski Federation that certain *loipes* should be reserved solely for this kind of step while it should be forbidden on other, more recreational *loipes*.

*The sheer pleasure of striding rhythmically through a peaceful valley **right**, with your body totally relaxed, your lungs relishing the crystal-clear air and your skis gliding gracefully over the snow, is difficult to match.*

This is the everyday pleasure of the cross-country skier, where distance ceases to be a consideration and the only limiting factor is the available daylight. Some Scandinavian sites even have lights.

CLOTHES
AND EQUIPMENT

*While there are no rules stipulating what you should wear for cross-country skiing **left**, there are a number of conditions which all suitable clothing should satisfy. Heavy and cumbersome clothing should be avoided if possible as should anything that restricts your body movement.*

There is no rule which states that the cross-country skier must conform to the accepted norms of Nordic dress. It is perfectly possible to ski in a pair of jeans and a sweater or even in a ski suit, but practice will rapidly demonstrate that this is not the most comfortable wear and that such garments are incompatible with the overall bodily freedom which cross-country skiing epitomizes. For this reason a very specific and universal garment selection has arisen which is not only comfortable but extremely stylish.

WHAT TO WEAR Light, wind-proof and snow-proof knickers are worn with knee-length woolen socks, topped by a matching blouse over a turtleneck shirt. The choice of underwear will depend very much on local weather conditions and for high-winter the customary light thermal underwear — undershirt and longjohns — are favored. In severe conditions, the addition of a light sweater may be necessary. The "anorak" top will usually have a kangaroo pocket but the trousers are mostly pocketless. For this reason, most cross-country skiers also wear a light rucksack to store essential personal items, possibly some food and, for most, a waxing and scraping set. Very few cross-country skiers go bare-headed and the traditional headgear is a close-fitting woolen cap without bobble or visor. Gloves are essential and while finger gloves give greater control and dexterity, mittens are perfectly acceptable. There is, however, an important point to watch here; as much work is done with hands and arms, the gloves should be comfortable, loose but not baggy and free of prominent seams around the base of the thumb and across the palm. Woolen gloves are acceptable but they wear out very quickly, while canvas and Gore-Tex-type outer gloves, although hard-wearing, do tend to slip. The ideal solution is wool reinforced by leather or pure leather, fleece-lined. For spring skiing gloves can be dispensed with.

The basic cross-country outfit should consist of either light, wind-proof and snow-proof knickers and knee-length woolen socks or (for more advanced skiers) a light-weight, one-piece tracksuit.

The knickers-and-sock combination can be worn with a matching blouse or turtleneck sweater, depending on personal preference.

Other vital accessories are a woolen cap or hat and gloves.

BOOTS Shoes or boots come in three basic designs. The lightest are very light and are really nothing more than running shoes. They are designed specifically for the high-performance skier and can be very cold and wet if the snow is deep. For the average cross-country skier a very light design of ankle-high boot, which gives adequate foot support while keeping out the worst of the snow, is the most popular. These are often fleece-lined for additional comfort. For those who intend to go for longer, rougher cross-country tours, there is a third type of boot, slightly heavier and higher and often worn with a second pair of short socks.

The fit and construction of all these types is extremely important. The act of skiing bends the boot or shoe to an acute angle with every step and this bend or fold occurs exactly above the middle joint of your big toe; poorly constructed boots will develop a permanent fold here which can become extremely painful and even disabling. Modern construction is such that the uppers are specially designed to prevent this happening but many cheaper versions are made without this provision. The fit should be comfortably snug: if the fit is loose, then the heel will move inside the shoe causing blisters; if the fit is too tight, then pressure on the toes, particularly the big toe, will result in bruising of the nail and very cold feet.

When purchasing cross-country boots, you will come across a special shoe designed for high-performance and racing skiing which incorporates a toe-tab onto which the binding will fit. This is *not* the shoe for the leisurely recreational skier. The normal cross-country shoe or boot is made to what is known as the "Nordic Norm," so that the soles will fit the standard binding, and there are specially prepared holes in the toe which fit the retaining spikes of the binding.

It is also important to see that the sole of the shoe or boot is suitable for walking on snow.

SKIS Cross-country skis are long, narrow and light. They are available in four basic designs: very narrow with special characteristics for racing purposes; slightly wider for "training" purposes, used by competitors for

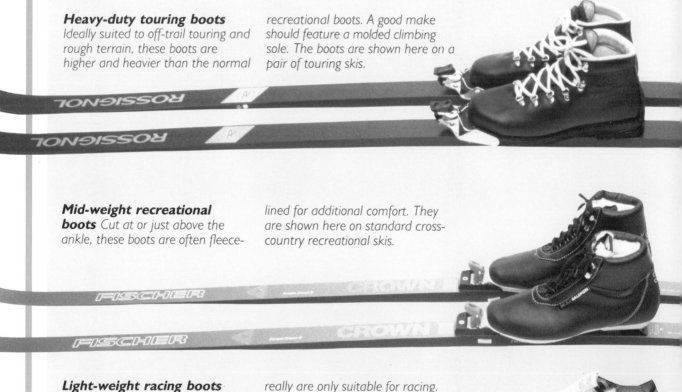

Heavy-duty touring boots
Ideally suited to off-trail touring and rough terrain, these boots are higher and heavier than the normal recreational boots. A good make should feature a molded climbing sole. The boots are shown here on a pair of touring skis.

Mid-weight recreational boots Cut at or just above the ankle, these boots are often fleece-lined for additional comfort. They are shown here on standard cross-country recreational skis.

Light-weight racing boots More like shoes than boots, these very light and low-cut shoes can get very cold and wet in deep snow and really are only suitable for racing. They are shown here on a pair of racing skis.

training and by enthusiastic amateurs with the technique to cope with the problems of this specialist type of ski; the "standard" cross-country ski, again slightly wider; and lastly, the touring type of ski, considerably wider and heavier, often with specially hardened or even steel edges and somewhat shorter and closer to an alpine ski.

The cross-country ski is constructed of a variety of wood laminates and plastic sandwiches, with the base covered by one of a variety of polyethylene base materials. The ski itself is long — in the region of 2 meters (approx. 2yd) — with a sharply upturned tip, a very pronounced arch or camber and little or no side-cut. The average weight of a pair (excepting the touring variety) is under 2lb 3oz, including the binding. The high arch is designed to facilitate the leg thrust and, at the same time, to provide a positive grip when fully weighted but to be just clear of the snow when gliding. These characteristics are decreased progressively as you move down the range of specialized models since the full use of the arch requires skilled techniques and lengthy practice.

Ski lengths *To choose the correct length of ski, stand with one arm raised and select the ski which reaches to your wrist. As a general guide, use the following figures: recreational skis — men 200—210cm, women 190—205cm; racing skis — men 210—215cm, women 200—210cm.*

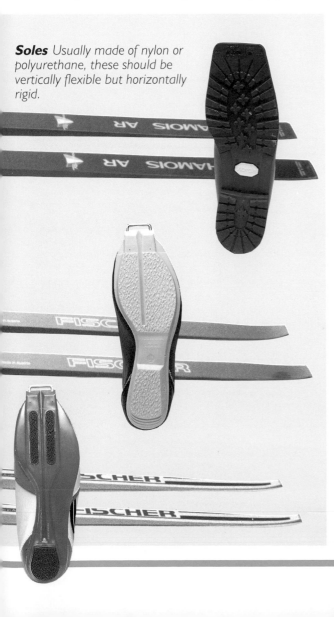

Soles *Usually made of nylon or polyurethane, these should be vertically flexible but horizontally rigid.*

161

WAX AND NO-WAX BASES The entire art of cross-country skiing depends upon the gliding/clinging propensity of the base. In conventional terms this is achieved by means of very skillful waxing techniques. However, recent technical innovations have reduced this problem for the recreational skier by means of special "no-wax" bottoms. These consist either of a fish-scale pattern embossed in the polyethylene base, the incorporation of narrow strips of nylon plush which will slide forward but resist backward movement or, not entirely satisfactorily, flakes or mica embedded in the base which have the same effect as the fish-scales or nylon strips. Most recreational skiers prefer one of the more sophisticated fish-scale bases, often restricted to the central part of the ski, despite the fact that in certain snow conditions this base pattern reduces the ease of gliding. It is, however, preferable to the skilled and time-consuming art of waxing.

BINDINGS Cross-country skis are held to the shoe by means of a simple and ingenious clamp, often called a "rat-trap." This consists of a very light aluminum frame which locates and centers the shoe while the actual binding clamps the shoe sole onto three spikes (which fit into the sole) by means of a simple ratchet device. The foot is completely free to lift but is limited in the degree of sideways movement by the side pieces of the toe frame. In addition to the front binding, it is common to incorporate a small olive-shaped device which fits into the heel of the shoe to prevent its moving sideways. A number of patents have also been taken out for more complicated designs, mostly consisting of a rail or V-shaped guide fitting into the heel of the shoe to achieve the same purpose. Touring skis are provided with very much heavier "rat-traps," though many touring skiers prefer a light type of cable binding derived from the old Kandahar cable binding.

SKI POLES Cross-country ski poles are long and light, and have a specially designed tip and basket which will not catch in the snow and a firm, comfortable handgrip with a relatively wide loop which is worn in the same manner as that for downhill skiing. Poles play a very important part in the overall skiing technique and contribute significantly to cross-country skiers' ability to propel themselves on snow. They should be chosen so

Wax and no-wax bases No-wax bases are a fairly recent innovation. On the standard touring ski **top** the fish-scale pattern extends along the whole length of the ski bottom, while on the recreational ski **center** the pattern is restricted to the central section. The racing ski **above** has a wax base which is divided into three areas

Touring, recreational and racing skis This side view of the three types of cross-country skis demonstrates the progressive reduction in arch or camber as you move from the racing ski **top** down to the touring ski **above**. The high arch distributes the skier's weight along the entire length of the ski

and provides a positive grip when fully weighted. On the touring ski steel edges are used to aid turning on rough terrain, and the ski is generally wider and heavier. Note also the sharply upturned tip on all three skis, a vital feature when lifting the ski during gliding.

that, when holding the pole by the handgrip with your arm extended sideways, your arm should be horizontal to the ground. The poles are made of fiberglass (with or without carbon fiber reinforcement), thin, light metal tubing, bamboo or occasionally in laminated, segmented tonkin.

WAXING Waxing is the esoteric side of cross-country skiing; entire books have been written on the subject and it is a perpetual topic for gossip, complaint, blame and argument. The theory underlying the problem is that you require a wax which when sliding forward will assist the gliding by providing a snow-proof, water-repellent surface but when pressed onto the snow, will collect enough snow crystals to prevent the ski from sliding backward. However, these crystals must instantly be brushed off the moment the ski is sliding. This is achieved by designing waxes of different hardness to suit differing snow crystals' consistencies. They are differentiated by color coding which relates to snow temperature, starting with violet at the warm end, graduating through red and blue to green at the extreme cold end. In addition it is customary to prepare

the front and back thirds of the ski with a gliding wax. The entire ski length is prepared with a hot-waxed base wax which, for downhill skiing, is scraped off to a micro-thin layer. The colored waxes ("climbing" waxes) are applied from the stick, lightly along the center third of the ski and then rubbed flat with a rubbing cork. All old wax is removed with a waxing torch and a cloth before applying new wax. Some skiers carry an armory of waxes and tools with them on a day's trip and will renew or change their wax every few hours. For the casual recreational skier there are much simpler waxes which consist either of three basic temperature colors or of a number of so called "universal" waxes which are said to be suitable for all types of snow and all temperatures. In addition, there are specialist "Klister" waxes; thick, glutinous and impossible to remove from clothes and hands, they are available in tubes. This wax is applied in a "buttering" motion with a wood spatula and is removed with a blow torch and old newspaper. Available in various temperature and snow-condition mixes, Klister is of particular value in warm, wet conditions and when other waxes appear not to work.

Ski poles Cross-country ski poles have a rather more comfortable handgrip **above** than downhill poles, and a very different basket design **below**. Most are asymmetric since they only need support you at the back.

163

RECREATIONAL CROSS-COUNTRY TECHNIQUES

The recreational skier need only acquire three skills: the ordinary walking glide (known as the "diagonal stride"); the double pole push; and the simplest method of turning corners, the stepped or skating turn.

The diagonal stride is the most effortless method of moving over flat or gently undulating ground using the glide efficiency of the ski propelled by alternate backward leg thrusts and alternate backward ski pole thrusts. It should be learned and practiced first by moving along a prepared flat track without poles. Swinging the arms as when walking, one ski should be thrust backward as if to push the other ski forward. The thrust or "kick" should be to the full extent of the leg's movement so that the heel actually lifts the tail of the ski off the ground and pivots it around the curve of the tip. Properly carried out this will produce a forward slide or glide which should not be allowed to run its full course — about one ski's length — before bringing up the trailing (unweighted) ski to the level of the leading foot, weighting it and almost simultaneously thrusting back with the previously leading leg.

During the course of the kick and glide, the body is leaned forward as if walking into a strong wind. Do not lift the ski forward in a kind of shuffle; the movement is a definite thrust backward followed by a swing of the same leg forward to a standing position.

Once this gliding walk has become easy and comfortable (it should be carried out slowly and rhythmically), the same track should then be practiced with ski poles but without moving the legs. The ski pole is grasped firmly and placed in the snow a short distance in front of the foot, the body is inclined forward and with body weight assisted by an arm push, the pole is pushed backward, causing the skis to glide forward. This should then be repeated with the other arm. With every kick the glide should not be allowed to finish before another pole push is started.

The third stage is to combine the leg thrust with the pole push. As in walking, the pole is inserted in front of the passive foot and as the other leg thrusts backward, the opposite pole and arm are pushed backward. The combined thrust of ski and pole will propel you forward for about two ski lengths. As the glide slows, the leg is swung forward together with the opposite arm while the new arm is used to plant the pole and, in time with the new leg thrust, push backward.

The diagonal stride should not be allowed to degenerate into a shuffle when the skis are moved forward and the poles only support your balance. The difficulty lies in balancing on one narrow ski during the glide when there is a tendency for the ski to tip sideways. To prevent this, make sure that you stand on the front of your gliding foot with toes splayed to counteract a tendency to sideways weighting.

At the end of each stride, the arm should be completely relaxed, the hand holding the pole barely grasping it and allowing the end of the pole thrust to be taken by the wrist strap around the back of your hand.

Gliding without poles Thrust one ski back **1** as if to push the other ski forward and swing your arms as if you were walking **2**, swinging the opposite arm forward to the ski being pushed back. The backward thrust should be extended until your heel lifts up. Allow the glide to run one ski's length **3** before repeating the sequence with your other leg, again swinging the opposite arm forward **4**. Lean your body forward in a dynamic stance and make sure that you thrust the ski back and slide it forward without lifting it off the snow.

Diagonal stride Repeat the "gliding without poles" exercise, but this time swing your arm forward **1** and plant the pole on the opposite side to the thrusting leg and level with your gliding foot **2**. Having planted the pole, synchronize the backward leg kick with an arm thrust on the pole **3**. Try and build up a nice rhythm so that you bring ski and opposite pole forward in tandem **4** during the glide phase and then repeat with the other ski and pole.

THE DOUBLE POLE PUSH

The double pole push is a technique employed mainly when the ground is slightly downhill. It is extremely simple and easy to learn. With both feet together, both poles are brought forward a short distance in front of the binding, the whole body weight is put on them and the upper body and legs are allowed to "collapse" onto the poles, pushing them backward to their fullest extent. At the end of this push, legs should be bent at the knee and the upper body should be leaning forward until the glide almost ceases, then the poles are swung forward, the body and legs straightened and a new push is started.

A common variant of the double pole push is the diagonal leg thrust combined with a double pole push. The legs can be alternated to avoid fatigue.

The double pole push is best suited to gentle downhill gradients. It can be used alone or in conjunction with a diagonal stride.

1 **Double pole push** Stand with both feet together and your knees lightly flexed.

2 Bring both poles forward, straighten your body and plant both poles halfway between your feet and your ski tips.

3 Bring your full body weight to bear on the planted poles and flex both knees.

4 Let your full body weight collapse onto your arms by flexing both knees deeply, and start pushing backward.

5 Keep pushing backward until your arms are fully extended.

6 During the glide phase bring both arms forward and straighten your knees.

1 ***Double pole push with diagonal stride*** *At the end of a diagonal stride, bring both arms forward and plant both poles.*

2 *Bring up the trailing leg and begin a normal double pole push.*

3 *Follow the push through until both arms are fully extended.*

4 *Bring both arms forward during the glide phase.*

5 *Thrust back with one leg as for a diagonal stride and bring both arms up for a double pole plant.*

6 *Plant both poles as for a double pole push and thrust back either with the same leg as before or alternate legs to avoid fatigue.*

7 *Synchronize the double pole thrust and diagonal leg kick so that both combine to propel you forward.*

8 *Use the end of the pole thrust as a resting phase for both arms and legs.*

9 *Use as much of the gliding phase as you can before making another pole and leg thrust.*

STEP TURNS

Turning corners on flat ground is carried out by means of step-turning. This consists quite simply of lifting the inside ski into the corner so that there is an angle of not more than 30 degrees between the skis. At the same time, the outside ski is used as a skate and pushes off sideways before being lifted back into line with the other ski. Depending upon the sharpness of the curve, this can be repeated several times in quick succession to achieve the new direction. The arm and pole movements are not interrupted and the thrust becomes a skating push.

On normal ground with a minimal gradient and where the double pole push or diagonal stride is being used, direction changes are made by stepping the inside ski progressively around the corner while using the outer ski as a skate.

*As you approach the corner **1**, start stepping your inner ski around. As the corner tightens, make bigger steps **4**, **5**, **6** and use your outer ski as a skate to keep your speed up. If necessary, additional speed can be gained by a vigorous thrust with the outer pole.*

MOVING UPHILL

Gentle slopes can be negotiated by the diagonal stride, but for anything steeper a form of climbing traverse or the herringbone must be used.

As in downhill skiing, there are essentially two methods for moving uphill on cross-country skis. Normal climbing wax or the no-wax bases will permit a climb of not more than about 15 degrees from the horizontal. On such a slope the diagonal stride will no longer glide and the overall stride must be shortened considerably to avoid undue fatigue. The skill lies in making best possible use of the adherence between ski and snow.

Walking uphill is rather like imagining your ski bases to be covered in tiny fish hooks. With each step you place the ski firmly on the snow without sliding and press it down into the snow as if you were making the fish hooks mesh into the snow surface. Each step must be well supported by the opposing pole which should carry most of your weight. Steps should be

4 Be sure to pick each ski up and forward so that both skis remain parallel.

5 Keep the uphill steps short and evenly spaced.

6 If the slope gets too steep you may have to revert to the normal side-step.

1 **Climbing traverse** Slide your upper ski uphill and forward, and support yourself on your lower pole.

2 Bring your lower ski uphill and forward to join your upper ski, and thrust off from your lower pole

3 Repeat the sequence, stepping uphill and forward, keeping your upper pole out of the way.

short and more rapid than the normal diagonal stride, as the ski will not hold a backward push for very long on a slope.

Do not force your way uphill in diagonal stride for longer than is comfortable. The moment the skis show any sign of slipping, revert to the standard herringbone.

When herringboning, remember that your skis are loose on your feet and you must not lift them up or they will dangle and not come to rest at the required angle. A cross-country herringbone is something of a shuffle rather than a series of distinct steps as is the case with the Alpine variation.

Normal herringbone When herringboning uphill you must remember to slide/shuffle each ski into position rather than lifting it. Try and push your knees into the slope so that each ski rests on its inside "edge," which helps stop it sliding backward. Plant alternate poles behind you and use them as both a support and thrusting platform.

Gliding or racing herringbone

This technique is particularly suited to slopes that are too steep for the diagonal stride but not so steep that no appreciable ground can be gained by sliding the skis forward. It is performed in exactly the same way as the normal herringbone except that the lower ski is used to provide a skating thrust (assisted by an alternate pole thrust) which actually propels the upper ski forward. Each thrust is repeated before the upper ski's gliding phase has stopped.

STEM/SNOWPLOW TURNS

Running downhill on cross-country skis presents a number of unexpected problems to the more experienced Alpine skier. The skis have virtually no lateral control and the heel being loose, no forward or turning pressures can be brought to bear (even though all the customary Alpine turns are open to the expert cross-country skier).

There are two common forms of braking and turning. The classic is the snowplow or stem. Applied to cross-country skis, it is a tiring but convenient form of slowing down and turning downhill corners, and is carried out as with Alpine skis but with one important difference — you must sit back on your heels at all times, otherwise the skis will run away with you. The braking and turning efficiency is thus greatly reduced and must be allowed for, and a certain amount of risk must be taken if the descent is in the customary prepared *loipe* grooves which will steer the skis as if on rails.

Both stem and snowplow turns are perfectly practical means of changing direction and reducing speed, but the actual technique differs slightly from that used in Alpine skiing.

5 *Because of the lack of real edges and the loose heel arrangement, control over the turn is not nearly as great as that experienced on Alpine skis.*

6 *To increase the degree of turn, increase the flex of your right knee and drop your right shoulder even further.*

7 *Unlike Alpine skis, cross-country skis will not run together after the turn, so you must slide your upper ski to join the lower ski, keeping your heels firmly weighted.*

1 As you approach your chosen turn location, slide your upper ski out.

2 Standing firmly on both heels, weight the upper ski by flexing your right knee and dropping your right shoulder.

3 As the skis begin to turn you must keep your full weight on your heels to stop the skis running away from you.

4 Allow the turn to continue gently, keeping your right knee flexed and your right shoulder dropped.

Braking snowplow Because of the absence of any real edges on cross-country skis, the efficiency of the braking snowplow technique is greatly reduced.

Keeping your weight firmly on both heels, slide both skis into a wide wedge position **1** and push both knees inward to tip the skis onto their inside "edges" **2**. Keep your arms by your sides throughout. To increase the braking efficiency, increase the inward flex of both knees and slide both skis into a wider wedge position **3**.

173

POLE BRAKING

Pole braking is a very handy alternative to stem or snowplow turns, especially when legs are tiring and courage is waning. The technique is carried out quite simply by taking both poles in one hand and holding them across your body (with knees bent) until the baskets drag in the snow. Increased braking is achieved by exaggerating the amount of body weight on the poles.

To turn corners using pole braking, simply turn the poles so that the baskets catch on the inside of the corner.

Joining the poles _Take both hands out of the pole straps and grip them together with one hand._

With your right hand grip the two handles together and move your left hand further down the poles.

Hold the poles diagonally across your body with the baskets resting lightly on the snow.

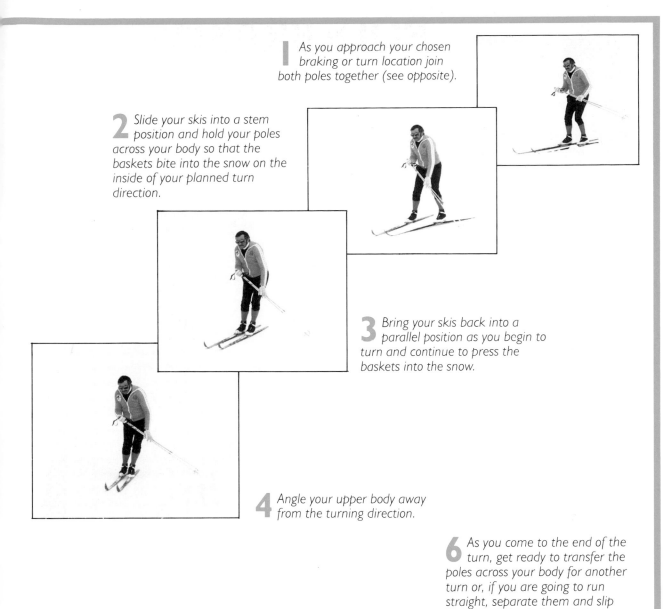

1 As you approach your chosen braking or turn location join both poles together (see opposite).

2 Slide your skis into a stem position and hold your poles across your body so that the baskets bite into the snow on the inside of your planned turn direction.

3 Bring your skis back into a parallel position as you begin to turn and continue to press the baskets into the snow.

4 Angle your upper body away from the turning direction.

6 As you come to the end of the turn, get ready to transfer the poles across your body for another turn or, if you are going to run straight, separate them and slip your hands back through the straps.

5 Push your knees into the turning direction and keep poles held diagonally across your body.

Competitive cross-country skiing is much more than the straightforward racing application of recreational techniques. The modern racing ski with its double tension arch or camber requires a highly sophisticated technique which the average recreational skier might never aspire to.

THE NORDIC EXTREMES

For all those who ski to enjoy the winter environment, there are those who ski for a different reason. For them skiing is not a therapy but a test, not a reward but a trial, not a question but an answer. They are the ski racers. According to Dr George Sheehan, an American sports medical consultant, the racers are looking for adventure within their own bodies. "The race was sport. It has a start, a finish, rules and officials. It begins and exists through the will and commitment of the athletes. It is life in a bounded situation, filled with effort and risk, uncertainty and tension. Here a decision to quit — of little account in a practice session — could become a statement of yourself, your character." Whatever the deeper psychological reasons, many recreational cross-country skiers sooner or later begin to think of their skiing in terms of times and performance, the first step towards actually competing.

RACING TECHNIQUES But the gap between racing and recreation is huge, and at the bottom of this mountain is technique. To begin with, although in modern racing it is not used to the extent it once was, the perfection of the conventional two-phase diagonal stride is a must. And to master this it is essential also that the specific techniques include the skill of using the modern competition ski with its double tension arch or camber. The purpose of this double or sequential camber is to provide a ski which when normally weighted runs mainly on the front and back of the skis while the center is barely in contact with the snow. When, however, a strong kick or push is applied, the ski flexes through the second, harder camber and makes firm contact with the snow thus enabling the wax to grip and provide full adhesion for the kick. It requires perfect technique to obtain a satisfactory thrust and glide with these advanced competition skis, but they do make the difference between good and poor times.

Conventional racing techniques do not differ from those used by the recreational skier, though side-by-side the single step-glide of the racer will outdistance that of the recreational skier by a couple of ski lengths. There is much more double poling and double pole, single step, diagonal stepping than used by the recreational skier and these tiring techniques are kept up for almost the entire length of the race — 9½mi, 18½mi or 31mi.

*The conservation of energy by removing unnecessary body movement is the hallmark of the advanced cross-country skier **right**. An interesting way to demonstrate this point is to study the upper body movements of a racer. Taken in isolation it would seem that the skier is virtually floating, propelled by an unseen force.*

THE SIITONEN STEP

The Siitonen step is, when reduced to its basic elements, nothing more than a double pole push combined with a very positive one-legged skating step.

The last two years of competitive skiing have seen the introduction — or more correctly the re-introduction after about 1,000 years of neglect — of the much discussed and controversial Siitonen step, the single ski skating step. This step involves lifting one ski out of the track and placing it at an angle of about 30-40 degrees to the other ski and in line with the center and, with a double pole push, skating the ski very hard backwards using the whole foot to push. This is repeated at every step. It is an exhausting technique which requires very special physical training and is inevitably going to result in specialist skis being developed, while encouraging a change in the ideal build of the cross-country skier from the customary light, slim, long-distance runner physique.

It is interesting to recall that the so-called asymmetric skis used throughout Scandinavia until late in the 19th century were viewed with curiosity and a certain disdain, while the reputed speeds achieved by skating one ski and gliding on the other were regarded as mythical. However, Norwegian research students carried out a series of tests on rebuilt archaic skis in the 1970s and confirmed the speed potential of the technique, but their findings attracted little attention until Siitonen, a Finnish cross-country specialist, put them into practice and the American cross-country team adopted the technique with devastating results for the conventional racers.

7 *Make sure you get full value from the pole push by thrusting your arms back until they are fully extended.*

6 *Repeat the skating push and double pole push.*

1 Lift your right ski out of the track and place it at an angle of about 30-40 degrees to your left ski. At the same time plant both poles as if for a double pole push.

2 Skate your right ski back vigorously and drop your body onto both poles to provide a strong double pole push.

3 As the glide progresses, lift the skated ski clear of the track.

4 Swing your right leg forward and at the same time bring your arms up for another pole plant.

5 Place your right ski back into the preparatory position and make a double pole plant.

179

THE CITIZEN MARATHONS

*The start of any citizen marathon is always a worrying time for competitors. In this start for the Finlandia Lahti Marathon **above**, some 10,000 skiers are all fighting for a track.*

The Nordic citizen long-distance races have a long and honorable history but only recently (coinciding with the growth of recreational skiing and the popular New York and London marathons) have they become mass participant events. Oldest and most famous of these races is the Vasaloppet in Sweden, 53½mi long and running from Salen to Mora. It celebrates the deliverance of Sweden from Denmark by Gustav Vasa in 1522, and was inaugurated in 1922 by Anders Pers, a Swedish journalist. Today almost 20,000 skiers take part in this grueling test of mind and limb and the winning time now stands at an incredible 3hrs 58 mins 88 secs (Konrad Hallenbarter in 1983). It is expected that with the new Siitonen technique this time will be considerably reduced.

An equivalent race is held annually in the USA. The American Birkebeiner (the original Birkebeiner race over 22mi is held annually in Norway from Guldbrandstal to Osterdal) was from the Telemark Ski Center to Hayward, Wisconsin, over a distance of 34mi.

The most popular of all these races is the Engadine Marathon from Maloja, through St Moritz to Zuoz, over a distance of 26mi which regularly has an entry of 20,000 competitors. It ranks as one of the most demanding of all these races, largely due to the extremely tricky ascent from St Moritz to the Staz lake and the long and difficult downhill section into Pontresina.

The longest of all the citizen marathons is the Canadian *Coureur de Bois* (Wood Runner) run over 100mi and lasting three days and two nights. It involves carrying a pack weighing a minimum of 11lb and containing a sleeping bag, overnight food and survival kit.

Entry to all these races is open to any skier, male or female, and entrants have to be sponsored by a nationally recognized ski club or federation. These popular citizen marathons have now spread to virtually every skiing country in the world and the FIS, reluctantly, now recognizes them as a distinct discipline and a form of World Cup points system operates to produce a world champion marathoner.

Participation in these races should not be taken lightly; a really good physical preparation must be undertaken and any potential competitor must make sure that he or she is actually capable of meeting the technical requirements and able to survive the distance. On the other hand it is not necesary to be a committed ski racer to partake; ordinary recreational equipment is perfectly adequate to bring home a respectable time. Nor is age a deterrent; 70- and 80-year-olds regularly compete and anyone who takes part and finishes within the maximum time allowed will take home a lasting memory of achievement.

The Engadine Marathon from Maloja to Zuoz enjoys probably the most beautiful scenery of all the marathons. Here some 15,000 skiers stream across the lakes to St Moritz, where the worst part of the course climbs over the hill and down to Pontresina.

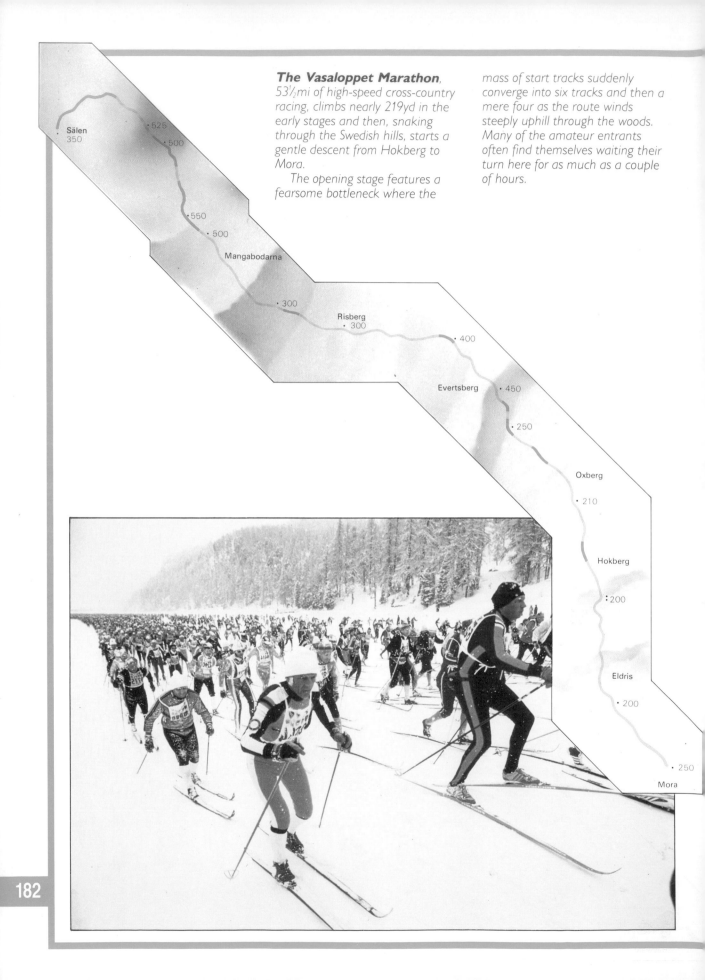

The Vasaloppet Marathon, 53½mi of high-speed cross-country racing, climbs nearly 219yd in the early stages and then, snaking through the Swedish hills, starts a gentle descent from Hokberg to Mora.

The opening stage features a fearsome bottleneck where the mass of start tracks suddenly converge into six tracks and then a mere four as the route winds steeply uphill through the woods. Many of the amateur entrants often find themselves waiting their turn here for as much as a couple of hours.

Sälen
350

• 525

• 500

• 550

• 500

Mangabodarna

• 300

Risberg
• 300

• 400

Evertsberg   • 450

• 250

Oxberg

• 210

Hokberg

• 200

Eldris

• 200

• 250

Mora

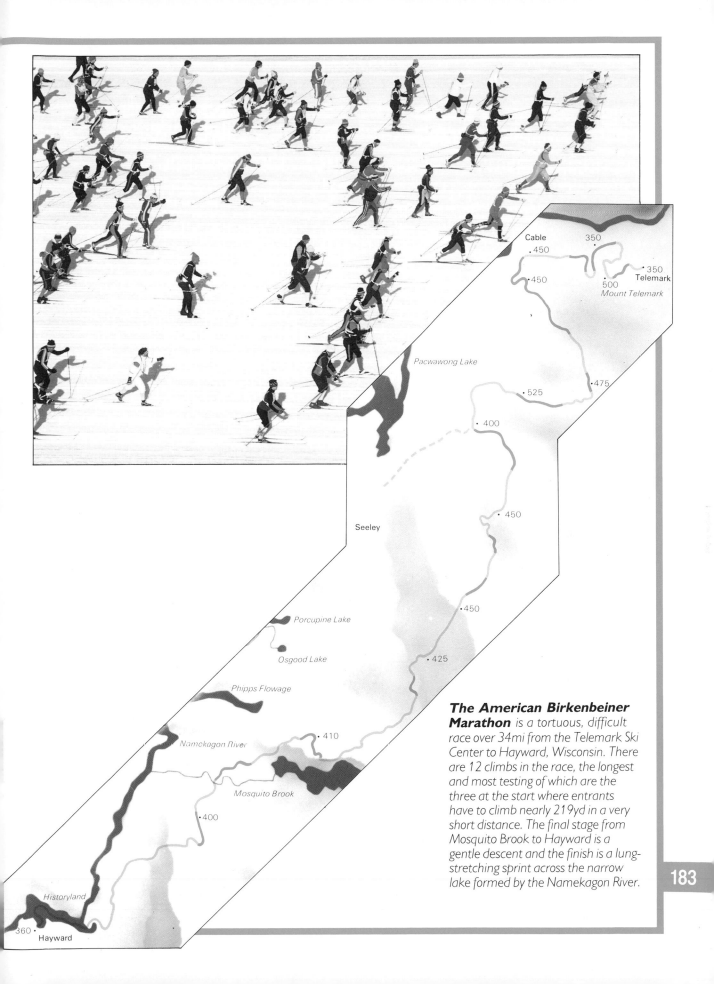

Cable
350
.450
.350
.450
500   Telemark
Mount Telemark

Pacwawong Lake

. 525
. 475

. 400

. 450

Seeley

. 450

Porcupine Lake

. 425

Osgood Lake

Phipps Flowage

. 410

Namekagon River

Mosquito Brook

. 400

The American Birkenbeiner Marathon is a tortuous, difficult race over 34mi from the Telemark Ski Center to Hayward, Wisconsin. There are 12 climbs in the race, the longest and most testing of which are the three at the start where entrants have to climb nearly 219yd in a very short distance. The final stage from Mosquito Brook to Hayward is a gentle descent and the finish is a lung-stretching sprint across the narrow lake formed by the Namekagon River.

183

Historyland

360 .
Hayward

NORDIC TOURING AND THE TELEMARK TURN

Nordic touring has always been part of the Scandinavian skiing scene, and notably in Norway there are some very large and exciting areas (for example the Vidda or Jotunheim) which provide week-long routes across the wild, empty plains and mountains, well provided with huts and shelters and marked routes. Similarly in Finnish Lapland there are organized treks of many days (complete with dog teams, Pulkas and overnight stops in Lap tents) which do not require more than conventional fitness and stamina. Increasingly this habit is spreading throughout North America, Canada and the Alps, and a whole line of specialized equipment has been developed.

For this kind of skiing a heavier, stronger boot is required and the skis resemble the release binding Alpine skis with a relatively broad footprint, reduced camber and noticeable side-cut. The bindings used are either specially strengthened "rat traps," or light Alpina- or Kandahar-type cable bindings. For most tours, waxing techniques are used rather than the no-wax bases, and in many cases, notably in the Alps, sticky skins are applied to the bases to assist climbing which are then removed for the descent.

The techniques required are still pretty basic and a sound performance of the stem and basic swing are the mainstay of the downhill progression. However, originating in the United States, that wonderful, beautiful, universal turn, the telemark, has made a revolutionary re-appearance, even to the point of specialist telemark-only downhill races.

Nordic touring, using rather heavier and sturdier skis than are used on prepared loipes, is the ultimate joy of recreational cross-country skiing. A tour can be anything from a day-long trek to the week-long expeditions so popular in Scandinavia. In the United States this discipline is becoming increasingly popular and there are many ambitious expeditions to be found on the long, linked trails in New England and the Rockies.

The growth of Nordic touring in the United States has also resulted in the revival of that most beautiful of all ski turns, the telemark **right, below***, first invented and perfected by Sondre Norheim more than a hundred years ago.*

TELEMARK TURNS The telemark is, fundamentally, a steered turn where one ski, the leading, outside ski, is in fact "carved" while the trailing ski is skidded. Ideally, the trailing ski follows the track of the leading ski so that the result is a single track turn, but this is an ideal which few can achieve and which, in fact, is an exaggeration of the basic telemark turn.

The turn is performed by advancing the outside ski to the point where the trailing ski foot is lifted by the heel and the trailing lower leg comes to lie parallel to the ski in a kneeling position. The leading ski is angled into the turn and edged. The arms are held loosely away from the body to balance the resulting turn but as the turn is initiated, the inside ski pole is pointed forwards and downwards (planted) as is the case in any Alpine parallel turn, providing a form of anticipation to the body which will help to initiate the turn. The angle of the leading ski determines the degree of turn and the degree of skid by the trailing ski. The turns are alternated by bringing up the trailing ski as the turn completes across the fall line and is advanced in one continuous movement to become the leading, steering ski.

This turn can be performed in any and every snow type but is particularly spectacular and effective in powder snow, and especially valuable in crud and crust as the surface is broken by the leading ski without any sudden collapse into the depth of the crust. To see two skiers linking telemark turns on a steep powder snow slope is one of the most beautiful sights in the ski world.

Although the telemark turn is ideally suited to powder snow **right**, *it is equally useful on hard-packed trail snow, crust and spring snow.*

1 Telemark turns *From a normal running position in an upright stance, bring your inner arm forward in anticipation of the pole plant.*

2 *Advance your outer, leading ski and place it at a slight angle into the direction of the turn while flexing your trailing knee so that your heel lifts clear of the ski.*

3 *Depending on the speed and tightness of the turn required, advance your leading leg so that your trailing shin is virtually parallel to the ground.*

4 As the turn gets underway, steered by your leading ski, spread your arms wide to help your balance and let your trailing ski passively follow your leading ski.

5 In theory the trailing ski should follow the exact path of the leading ski, but in practice it is usually allowed to skid a little wide.

6 At the end of the turn, bring your trailing ski up parallel with the leading ski and, if a second turn is required, advance it forward to steer a new turn.

187

INDEX

Numbers in *italics* refer to illustrations.

absorbing a jump 98
accessories 20
Adler 151
advanced intermediate
    96
advanced parallel turns
    110
advanced short swing
    108, *108-9*
Aiguille du Tour *150*
Aiguilles Doré 151
Allais 10
Alpine-type cable
    bindings 184
Alpine ski slopes 68
    ski races 124
American Birkebeiner
    marathon 180, *183*
American cross-country
    team 178
American method
    (ATM) 12, 64, 130
angulation *66, 67,* 102
Anorak 16
anticipation, *67, 67,* 90
apprentice teachers 10
Argentière, France *150,*
    151
Arlberg 10, 14
Arlberg School 10
Arrow, See FLECHE
    artificial snow 39
ATM. See AMERICAN
    TEACHING METHOD
Audi Ski Guide 33
Austrian teaching 10-11
avalanches 146-7
    dry, powder snow
        147
    slab 147
    wet snow slides 147
avalanche victims 147
avalement 98, 110, *110-*
    111

backpack *23*
banked parallel turns
    116, *116-7*
bases 16
    wax and no-wax 162
basic closed parallel 102,
    102-3, 104
basic exercises 30
basic short swings 104,
    104-5
basic swing 64, 73
basic turn 64, 73
beginnings, the 10
beginner's slopes 32, 35
bending *66, 67*
Bilgeri 10
binding dynamics 28
bobble hat *21*
boot bag *23*
boot controls *25*
boots 160
Bourg St Pierre *150,* 151
braking plow 56, *56, 173*
bronze badge 13
bumps and hollows 12,
    68-9, 68-9
bumps and jumps 98
bump swallowing 129

Cabane de Chanrion *152*
Cabane des Dix *153*
Cabane de Vignettes
    150
cable-cars, 34, *35*
carving 12, *67,* 114, *114-*
    15
categories of skiers 13

Cathomen, Conradin *127*
Caulfield, Vivian 10
chair-lift 12, 34-5, *34*
Chamois series 15
Chamonix, France 151
Champex *150,* 151
children's races 15
children's ski school
    classes 11
choosing skiwear 18
Christiania 10
citizen marathons 180
climbing 12, 39, 50, *50-1*
climbing traverse *169*
clip boots 16
closed stance *66, 67*
clothes 16-17
Col du Mont Brulé 152,
    152, 153
collar *19*
comfort warranty 25
comma position 11, 59
compression turn 110
conduct at accidents 39
conjunctivitis 23
controlling a jump *100- 1*
control of direction 38
control of speed and
    skiing 38
counter-rotation 90
Coureur de Bois 180
course marshals 126
crampons 148
cross-country
    bindings 162
    skier *177*
    skiing 154-87
    ski poles 162-3, *163*
    skis 160-1
crust 141
cuffs *19*
Curran, Jim 35

Das ganze Volk fährt Ski
156

Das Wunder des
    Schneeschuhs 10
Davos 33, 34
deep snow *144*
diagonal stride 164, *165*
DIN (German Industrial
    Standards
    Association) 28
double pole push 128,
    164, 166, *166*
    with diagonal stride
        167
downhill racing 124
downhill course *127*
down-ski stem turns 12
down-stem 73

Ecole de Ski France
    (ESF) 14, 15
edge 67
Einsiedeen hills 156
elasticized waistband *19*
electronic timing 126,
    128
Emahusen, Jens 10
emergency telephone
    positions *127*
Engadine Marathon 180,
    181
equipment 16-17, 24-9
equipment, renting 24
ESF. See ECOLE DE SKI
    FRANCE
European trail maps *37*
expert 96
expert class 13
eyes 22-3

PICTURE CREDITS

Quarto Publishing would like to thank the following for permission to reproduce copyright material (abbreviations used — *t:top, l:left, r:right, b:bottom, c:centre):*

Allsport   16 122 123 157 158 176 180 181 182 183

J Allan Cash 32 33 152 153

Daniel Rose 11 17 18 34 35 (t,b) 121 124 125 126 (t,b) 127 128 (t,c,b) 129 130 131 (t,c,b) 132 135 140 142 144 (t) 147

Barry Smith 14/15 38 136 139 141 (t,c,b,) 143 144 (c,b) 145 (t,c,bl,br) 146 149 (r) 155 184 185

Spectrum   13

ACKNOWLEDGMENTS

Quarto Publishing would like to thank the following for their assistance in the research and production of this book:

British Association of Ski Instructors (BASI)
Roy Bisset
Doug Godlington
Pixie Maynard
David Goldsmith
Alpine Sports Ltd
Katie Tanner